SCIENCE EXPERIM
FOR SMART KIDS

Over 101 Awesome at Home Science Experiments for Children.
Turn your Kitchen or Outdoor Space into a Mad Lab!
(STEAM Activities for Kids 3+)

ModernQuill
Education

ModernQuill Education

TABLE OF CONTENTS

HOW TO USE THIS BOOK

Today science has taken a huge place in our everyday lives from the salt we eat to the car we use, everything is made with some scientific chemistry.

Let us look at a few examples:

The Earth we walk on is due to gravitational force by which Earth attracts us and we are able to walk on it comfortably. We might take it for granted, but, other planets lack it.

The house you're living in is also made with a little hint of science. As all the machines and material used in making is a revolutionary invention of science.

Without science in our lives there would be no advancement in our world. Whether it's the smart phones we're on daily or the everyday lightbulb – it's clear that our everyday life heavily relies on modern day science.

In order to bring more comfort and innovations into our lives, it's essential that we as parents teach our children some exciting science! As maybe they can help innovate and pave the path for modern science!

Many of the experiments are very easy to carry out and are guaranteed to be a blast. Some of the experiments require a parent's or adult's supervision (which we carefully noted for your little one's safety!) But the #1 rule is always to have fun with this book!

NOTE TO PARENTS

This book is designed to inspire your little one's creativity side while teaching them the basics of everyday modern science using basic household items.

Many of the experiments are very easy to carry out whereas a few of them need parent's or adult's supervision – however we duly noted them to help keep safety the #1 priority.

As we all know that children these days are so much into digital world of gadgets and they spend a very less time doing some physical and creative work. Please use this book as both an educational and relationship bonding tool.

We created this book to explain the importance of science, but also as a learning tool for your little one's. We've made it so entertaining that your little one's won't even realize that they're learning!

Last but not least, this book will help them logically brainstorm, inspire creativity and demonstrate teamwork & communication skills. All are arguably very important in the modern world,

EXPLAINING THE SCIENTIFIC METHOD

What is the Scientific Method?

The scientific method is as a strategic method of research in which a problem is identified, data is gathered, a hypothesis is formulated from this data, and the hypothesis is scientifically tested with observations duly recorded.

In simpler terms, the scientific method is a way for scientists to study and learn new things. It doesn't matter what the scientist is trying to learn, using the scientific method can help them come up with an answer to problem!

The History of the Scientific Method

The scientific method wasn't invented by one person, but was developed by several different scientists over the years. Francis Bacon, Rene Descartes, and Isaac Newton all helped contribute to the development of the scientific method in an effort to help better understand nature and science.

Scientific Method Steps

The scientists mentioned above, were able to create a simple six step process in which how to test common problems and discover a plausible answer! The six steps below go as followed:

1. Ask a question

2. Gather information and observe

3. Make a hypothesis

4. Experiment and test your hypothesis

5. Analyze your test results

6. Present a conclusion

Why is the Scientific Method Important?

In conclusion, the scientific method is the staple better understanding modern science. Without a formal method of determining questions and their answers, we wouldn't have the everyday science or the knowledge we have today that often we take for granted!

1.   Glow In The Dark Ice Cubes

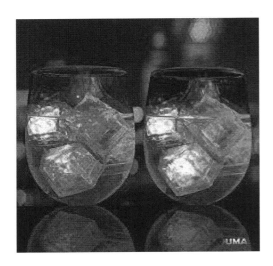

Have you ever tried to make something that glows at home? Well, it isn't a difficult task to do. All you have to do is use a magical ingredient for it which in this case is tonic water. It will help in making the ice cubes glow.

Things You'll Need:

- Ice Cubes
- Tonic Water
- Food Color
- Water
- Black Light
- Fluorescent Fabric Color

The Procedure:

Step 1:

Take some normal water in a beaker and pour it in ice tray to freeze. Repeat the same for tonic water and also put it in the freezer.

Step 2:

Now put some food color and fluorescent fabric color in both trays and then let them freeze again.

Step 3:

After taking out the trays from the freezer turn off the lights and flash some black light on the ice cubes in both trays. You'll see the ice cubes glowing in one of the trays i.e. the one containing tonic water.

How It Works:

The magical compound quinine contains a highly fluorescent compound which helps the things to glow in dark. That is the reason for glowing of the ice cube made from tonic water.

Precautions For Safety:

- Do not directly look into the black light as it is harmful for the eyes.

- Do not use acrylic colors as they are not edible.

Observations:

_____

_____

_____

2. Marbled Paper

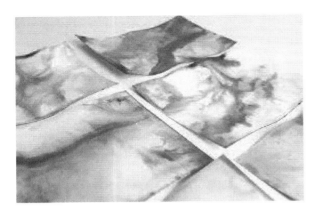

Do you want to make some exciting marbled papers from milk? If yes then follow the procedure below.

Things You'll Need:

- Almond Milk
- Dish Soap
- Toothpicks
- Water Color Papers
- Tray
- Food Coloring or Water Colors with Dropper

The Procedure:

Step 1:

Take a tray related to the size of paper which you're going to use. Put some milk into it which covers the floor of the tray and add some drops of different food or water colors randomly.

Step 2:

Now add the little chunks of dish soap randomly and mix it a little with toothpicks.

Step 3:

Before the colors get too mixed lay down the paper on the tray and press gently.
Now put the paper aside and let it dry.
Repeat the same with all water color papers you have.

How It Works:

The colors and soap chunks mixed together will make cute and amazing patterns on the papers having unique designs.

Precautions for Safety:

- Do not put anything in mouth as this is not an edible experiment

Observations:

_____

_____

_____

3. Orange Fizz

Have you ever felt fizzy bubbles in your mouth? If not then follow this crazy experiment to feel the fizz of oranges.

Things You'll Need:

- An Orange
- Half Teaspoon Baking soda

Step 1:

Cut the orange into sections.

Step 2:

Dip a slice or section of orange into the bicarbonate of soda.

Step 3:

Take a bite. As you chew, it should start to bubble/fizz in your mouth.

How It Works:

When acids and bases mix, you get some exciting chemistry! Oranges and other citrus fruits are crammed with acid. It's a secure acid, and it's what gives oranges, lemons, and limes their sourness. Bicarbonate of soda may be a base, the other of an acid. It's also safe, but doesn't taste excellent on its own, and can offer you a tummy ache if you eat tons of it. Because the acid and bicarbonate of soda mix, it makes many CO_2 bubbles, an equivalent gas you exhale, and therefore the same one that creates soda so fizzy.

Precautions for Safety:

- Avoid using so much of baking soda as it is not so good for eating raw.

Observations:

_____

_____

_____

4. Storm In A Glass

A wonderful cloudy storm closed in a glass of water with some spread over food colors making the sight even more wonderful.

Things You'll Need:

- Water
- Shaving Cream
- Food Coloring
- A Large Glass
- A Spoon

The Procedure:

Step 1:

Fill the glass half full with water

Shower some shaving cream on head of the water to fill the glass to ¾ full.

Step 2:

Utilize your finger or a spoon to spread the shaving cream equitably over the head of the water. The head of the shaving cream ought to be level.

Step 3:

Blend ½-cup water with 10 drops of food shading in a different compartment. Delicately include the shaded water, spoonful by spoonful, to the head of the shaving cream. At the point when it gets excessively substantial, watch it storm!

How It Works:

Mists in the sky clutch water. They can hold a large number of gallons! The layer of shaving cream is our imagine cloud in this trial. The shaving cream layer can likewise clutch water. Mists can't continue putting away increasingly more water everlastingly, in the long run they get excessively substantial. At the point when that occurs, the water drops out (hastens) as downpour, day off, or hail.

Precautions for Safety:

Be careful while using shaving cream.

Observations:

_____

_____

_____

5. Moldy Apples

Watch apples decay in different ways using three different fluids.

Things You'll Need:

- 1 Apple Cut Into 4 Equivalent Pieces
- 4 Bricklayer Containers
- Vinegar
- Salt Water
- Lemon Juice

The Procedure:

Step 1:
Put an apple piece in every holder.

Step 2:

Fill every holder most of the way with one of the fluids. Ensure the apple piece is shrouded in the fluid. The fourth apple and holder is your benchmark group, so don't add anything to that one.

Step 3:

Save the containers in cool territory for seven days. Watch apples for decay, form, and some other changes.

How It Works:

Microscopic organisms want to develop on things like natural product. At the point when you put natural product in the cooler, the chilly temperature hinders the procedure. Be that as it may, in this analysis the organic product is presented to room temperature. Salt is a characteristic preserver since it got dried out the water from the apple, lessening the zone where microorganisms can develop and flourish. Then again, the lemon juice was an ideal play area for microbes to play in view of the sugar.

Precautions for Safety:

Don't cut the apples yourself as you can harm yourself.

Observations:

_____

_____

_____

6. Volcano Steam

An experiment of acid-base reaction turning out into a volcano.

Things you will need;

- A Bowl
- Golf ball
- Preparing Soda
- Water
- Food Coloring (Optional)
- Vinegar
- Cling Wrap
- Blade (Parent Supervision Recommended)
- Pipette
- Cooler

The Procedure:

Step 1:

Put golf ball in a vacant bowl.
Wrap plastic fold around golf ball and bowl with the goal that the golf ball is secured and plastic wrap comes out over the sides of the bowl.

Step 2:

Make a blend of water and heating soft drink that will top off the remainder of your bowl. The blend is 2/3 water, 1/3 preparing pop. You can likewise include 3 drops of your preferred food shading. This blend will sit on head of the cling wrap. You need to ensure the blend covers the golf ball totally.
Put bowl in cooler.

Step 3:

When solidified, let defrost a bit. At that point, flip over bowl and take out your frigid spring of gushing lava. Use quality, scissors, or your fingers to get plastic wrap off as most ideal as. You can let your grown-up chief assistance you with getting this show on the road golf ball out. Might need to have a go at utilizing a blade for this part.
Head outside and utilize your pipette to do a spurt of vinegar into your cold fountain of liquid magma and see what occurs!

How It Works:

In science, when you have a corrosive and a base together, they can eject in your face. The heating soft drink in the blend was the base, and the vinegar is a corrosive. So when combined they have a compound response and discharge carbon dioxide. Cool! Truly Cool!

Precautions for Safety:

Do not use knife yourself alone without adult supervision.

Observations:

_____

_____

_____

7. Drifting Egg

What happens when you put an egg in a glass of ordinary water? floating-egg

This is a cool method to find out about thickness.

Things you will need;
- One Egg
- A Spoon
- Tall Drinking Glass
- 1-2 Cups of Salt
- Water

The Procedure:

Step 1:

Empty water into the glass until it is about half full. Spot an egg in the glass of water and check whether it sinks or buoys (it should sink).

Step 2:

Mix in loads of salt. Start with 1 tablespoon and mix it until the salt breaks up. Continue including increasingly salt until the egg coasts.

Step 3:

Next, cautiously pour all the more new water until the glass is about full (be mindful so as to not upset or blend the pungent water in with the plain water). In case you're cautious, you can get the egg to coast between the new and saltwater!

How It Works:

The egg is denser than water (more atoms per square inch), this makes it sink. At the point when you begin dissolving salt in the water, this is expanding the thickness (including more particles per square inch). In the long run the water gets denser than the egg making the egg drift. At the point when you cautiously include new water once more, this new water is less thick than the salt water so it skims directly on top!

Observations:

_____

_____

_____

8. Bendy Bones

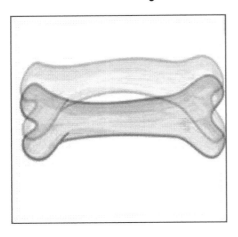

Things You'll Need:

- 2 Glass jars
- Water
- Vinegar
- Turkey Bones
- A Writing Utensil
- 2 Labels

The Procedure:

Step 1:
Gather turkey bones from Thanksgiving supper and wash them.

Step 2:
Empty water into one container and vinegar into the other one.

Name the containers so you know which one is which.

Step 3:

Spot turkey bones into containers and leave for seven days.
Flush off bones and attempt to twist them. Which ones curve simpler?

How It Works:

Bones are loaded up with calcium carbonate. At the point when calcium carbonate responds to the vinegar it debilitates the bones. Bones need calcium to remain solid, however when it gets modified it gets frail and bendy.

Observations:

_____

_____

_____

9. Dry Erase Magic

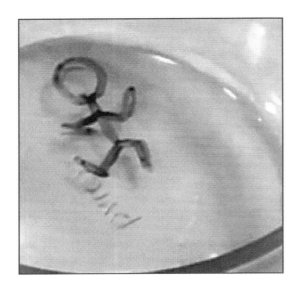

To create a stick figure which goes from static to motion in 3 simple steps.

Things you will need;
Glass
A bowl
A Dry Erase marker
Water

The Procedure:

Step 1:

Draw a basic picture on the bottom of a bowl. A stick figure is a decent one to begin with.

Step 2:

Pour water into the bowl gradually to lift up the drawing.

Step 3:
Whirl the water around to make the image move and dance.

How It Works:

The marker deserts blend of colors and a sort of liquor combined. The liquor breaks up and the colors are deserted as a strong. Glass is smooth to such an extent that the stick figure made slides directly off when it gets wet!

Observations:

_____

_____

_____

10. Hovering Ping Pong Ball

This experiment will show you how to move a ping pong ball in air without any strings attached.

Things You'll Need:

- Hair Dryer
- Ping Pong Ball

The Procedure:

Step 1:

Set the hair dryer to blow simple air rather than warmed air. A warmed hair dryer will work if your dryer doesn't have this choice.

Step 2:

Hold the ping pong ball simply over the spout of the hair dryer and turn broadcasting in real time. Let the ping pong ball go, and it should glide over the spout.

Step 3:

Attempt various settings to check whether you can get the show on the road to coast higher.

Tilt the hair dryer a tad from one side to the next. Does the ball despite everything skim?

How far would you be able to tilt the dryer before the ball tumbles to the floor?

How It Works:

As the hair dryer blows air around the ping pong ball it creates areas of high pressure and low pressure. Where there is high pressure it pushes the ball into the middle and where there is low pressure the ball just stays to there.

Precautions for Safety:

Don't let the child use dryer alone. As it will be connected to some electric supply.

Observations:

_____

_____

_____

11. Lava Lamp

You can make your own Lava Lamp at home with some household items.

Things You'll Need:

- Plastic bottle
- Water
- Food Coloring
- Fizzy Tablets (Alka Seltzer)
- Vegetable Oil

The Procedure:

Step 1:
Top the container off around 1/fourth (1 quarter) with water. Pour the vegetable oil in the container until is practically full. You might need to utilize an estimating cup with a spout or a pipe.

Step 2:
Include a couple of drops of your preferred food shading. Watch as the shading sinks through the oil. Did your drops of shading blend in with the water quickly or skim in the middle of for a couple of moments?

Step 3:

Break your bubbly tablet down the middle and drop some portion of it into the container. Prepare … here come the bubbly masses! You can even get a spotlight, turn off the lights and drop in another half tablet. This time sparkle the electric lamp through the flashlight while the masses are foaming!

How It Works;

The oil coasts on head of the water since it is less thick or lighter than water. The food shading has a similar thickness as the water so it sinks through the oil and blends in with the water. At the point when you add the tablet it sinks to the base at that point begins to break down. As it breaks down it makes gas, carbon dioxide. Gas or air, is lighter than water so it buoys to the top. The air bubbles carry some hued water with them to the top. At the point when the air comes out of the shaded water mass, the water gets substantial again and sinks. It does this again and again until the tablet is totally broken down.

Observations:

_____

_____

_____

12. Spooky Jack-O-Lantern Volcano

Turn a pumpkin into a Jack O Cano.

Things You'll Need:

- A Small Pumpkin
- Vinegar
- Baking Soda
- Dish Soap
- Food Coloring
- Water
- Plastic Container

The Procedure:

Step 1:

With parent management, wipe out pumpkin all things considered. Spot pumpkin onto plastic holder so ejection doesn't cause a major jumble.

Step 2:

Fill pumpkin with 3/4 brimming with water.
Include 10 drops of food shading.
Include 4-5 drops of dish cleanser.

Include 1/4 cup vinegar.

Step 3:
At the point when you are prepared for it to detonate, include the heating pop and appreciate!

How It Works:

At the point when you join a base (preparing pop) and a corrosive (vinegar) together you make a substance response where carbon dioxide is made and discharged. This in a huge amount, makes a bubbly burst or ejection.

Precautions for Safety:

Avoid contact of vinegar with your eyes.

Observations:

_____

_____

_____

13. Super Cool Soda

Make a Slushy Soda at Home!

Things You'll Need:

- A Glass
- Soda

The Procedure:

Step 1:
Put the container of soda into the freezer for 45 minutes. Hold up 45 minutes.

Step 2:

Test to check whether it is super cooled: put an ice 3D square in a glass and spill somewhat fluid out of the container. On the off chance that it is super cooled, it will turn the consistency of a milkshake.

Step 3:

In the event that it is still totally fluid, set the jug back into the cooler with the top screwed on for 15 minutes.

Rehash stages 3 and 4 until you have a supercool treat. In the event that your jug freezes strong in the cooler, you can attempt the reinforcement bottle (on the off chance that you utilized two containers) or run the solidified jug under warm water until it defrosts.

How It Works:

Water freezes at 32 degrees Fahrenheit, 0 degrees Celsius. It is conceivable to bring it under 32 degrees F, yet normally just for a brief period, and just if there are no ice precious stones shaped in the water yet. Once the supercool water shapes a precious stone or contacts another bit of ice, it freezes in a rush!

Observations:

_____

_____

_____

14. Golden Pot

Make golden pot at home using some chocolate coins.

Things You'll Need:

- Paper Plates
- Chocolate Coins
- Stop Watch
- Pen
- Paper
- Black Marker
- Plastic Cup

The Procedure:

Step 1:
Remove the foil from every chocolate coin you use for the analysis. Spot every chocolate coin on a different paper plate. Spot paper plates in various spots, for instance, one outside in the shade, one outside in the sun, one inside in a dim room, or one inside under a light.

Step 2:
At every area, place up to 3 plates to see which softens the quickest:
1 white paper plate with simply the chocolate coin.
1 white paper plate, with an unmistakable plastic cup over it, covering the coin to permit it to trap some warmth.

1 paper plate, shading the plate dark with a marker, to check whether this assimilates more warmth.

Step 3:
Utilizing your stop watch, pen, and paper, record to what extent it takes the chocolate to dissolve in every circumstance. On the off chance that it doesn't soften after 10 min of sitting, record that also.
Look at your outcomes and consider the end to your outcomes.

How It Works:

At a specific temperature a portion of your chocolate coins experienced a physical change from a strong to a fluid. This procedure is called dissolving. Vitality was added to the chocolate by either daylight or warmth and this vitality caused the atoms that make up the strong chocolate to move about and spread out and turn into a fluid.

Precautions for Safety:

Do not use flame for warming the chocolates as you can harm yourself.

Observations:

_____

_____

_____

15. Liquid Layers

Have you ever noticed that some liquids mix and some don't?
This simple experiment will help you know that.

Things You'll Need:

- Vegetable Oil
- Syrup
- Food Coloring
- Paper Towels
- Tall Glass
- A Large Spoon
- Water

The Procedure:

Step 1:
Fill the glass most of the way with ordinary water. Include a drop of food shading, in the event that you have some convenient. Be mindful so as not to include excessively or you probably won't have the option to perceive what is occurring.
Step 2:

Gradually empty a portion of the syrup into the water and see what occurs. Does it sink or buoy?

Step 3:

Gradually include a portion of the oil. It is a smart thought to hold the spoon simply over the water level, contacting the side of the glass, at that point gradually pour the oil onto the spoon. Does the oil sink or buoy?

How It Works:

Every one of these fluids has various densities (the measure of particles per square inch). The denser fluids have more particles; this makes them sink to the base. The less thick fluids drift.

Precautions for Safety:

Do not use any other liquid than suggested.

Observations:

_____

_____

_____

16. Real Life Butter Fingers

Yummy for your tummy butter fingers.

Things You'll Need:

- 1/2 Cup of Whipping Cream
- 8-Ounce Screw-Top Plastic Compartment or Artisan Container
- 1/4 Teaspoon of Salt (optional)
- Spoon

The Procedure:

Step 1:

Empty whipping cream into screw-top plastic compartment. (try not to fill more than midway)
Include Salt.
Step 2:

Ensure you screw the top on close. Shake for 7-9 minutes or until the cream quits sloshing around and you are left with a yellow mass.

Step 3:

Shake for a couple of moments longer. Congrats! You have unadulterated spread. Presently you can serve it at any occasion!

How It Works:

As you stir whipped cream, you beat beads of butterfat until they crumple and rejoin to shape a solitary mass of spread. This is a case of emulsion, where one fluid balances suspended in another.

Precautions for Safety:

An edible experiment with no precautions.

Observations:

_____

_____

_____

17. Homemade Play Dough

Every kid loves to play with a play dough, so why not to make it at home.

Things You'll Need:

- Flour 3 Cups
- Salt One and a Half Cup
- Water 3 Cups
- Cream of Tartar 6 Tablespoons
- Oil 3 Tablespoons

The Procedure:

Step 1:
Break down salt in the water.
Empty all fixings into a huge pot.

Step 2:

Mix continually over medium warmth until a ball structures by pulling endlessly from the sides.
Massage the batter blend until the surface matches play dough (1-2 minutes).

Step 3:

Store in plastic compartment.

How It Works:

The floor helps in making dough very easily at it has the same texture.

Precautions for Safety:

Simple experiment with no harm.

Observations:

_____

_____

_____

18. Over the Rainbow

Follow the steps below to make a cute rainbow in a glass!

Things You'll Need:

- Dropper
- Spoon
- Water
- Mug
- Separate Mugs (5)
- A Glass

The Procedure:

Step 1:
Separate the Skittles into cups, in the sums: 2 red, 4 orange, 6 yellow, 8 green, and 10 purple.
Warmth a cup of water in the microwave for a moment and a half (not bubbling).
Be cautious expelling the water from the microwave–it's hot!

Step 2:
Quantify and pour two tablespoons of high temp water into each cup, on head of the Skittles.

Mix each cup cautiously so no water sprinkles out. The cups should be cool for the following piece of the examination, so leave them some place where they won't get thumped over. Mix them at regular intervals or so until the Skittles are broken down and the water is room temperature.

Step 3:
Utilizing the dropper, include the hued water from the five cups to the unmistakable glass. Start with purple, at that point include green, at that point yellow, orange, and red last. Go gradually here, we don't need the various layers to blend.
Congrats, you made a rainbow. You didn't need to head outside now!

How It Works:

Skittles are generally made of sugar. At the point when you add high temp water to them, the sugar breaks up and the shading on the shell of the Skittles turns the water various hues. The cup with just two red Skittles doesn't have as much sugar as the cup with ten purple Skittles, however the two of them have a similar measure of water. The measure of issue pressed into a specific measure of room is known as the thickness of the material. The red water is less thick than the purple water, so it will skim on head of the purple water.

Precautions for Safety:

Boil the water under adult supervision as you can burn yourself.

Observations:

_____

_____

_____

19. Invisible Extinguisher

Things You'll Need:

- Tall Glass or Plastic Cup
- Lighter
- Short Glass or Plastic Cup
- Tea Light

The Procedure:

Step 1:
Spot tea lights in the short drinking glass. Utilizing a security lighter, light the tea lights while leaving them in the glass
In the tall glass, pour 1/2 cup vinegar.

Step 2:
Gradually sprinkle 1/2 tablespoon of heating soft drink into the tall glass containing the vinegar. You can dump it all in without a moment's delay, however be prepared for a major ejection! Let the response delayed down until the froth has vanished.

Step 3:

Tilt the tall glass on its side over the tea light as though you were pouring the air over it. In the event that the fire doesn't go out on your first attempt, pour another scoop of preparing soft drink into the vinegar and rehash stages 5 and 6.

How It Works:

The preparing pop/vinegar response brings about a gas called Carbon Dioxide (CO_2). CO_2 is more thick than typical air, which implies that it will sink! Since CO_2 sinks, it remains in the cup as opposed to coasting endlessly like an ordinary blend of air would. This implies you have a cup loaded with CO_2!

The flame consumes on account of a burning response that requires Oxygen (O_2), something we find in plenitude noticeable all around us. At the point when you empty your cup of CO_2 into the cup containing the light, the CO_2 sinks to the base of the cup and encompasses the flame. This uproots (or pushes up) all the regularly blended air, alongside all that O_2 the fire needs to consume. Furthermore, Voila! Your flame is stifled imperceptibly!

Precautions for Safety:

Use lighter under supervision.

Observations:

_____

_____

_____

20. Paper Airplane

Things You'll Need:

- A Square Paper

The Procedure:

Step 1:

Start by collapsing the square into equal parts corner to corner to make a triangle. Crease that triangle into equal parts corner to corner to shape a littler triangle.

Step 2:

Unfurl the past crease to get the bigger triangle. Overlap the edges of the triangle into the recently made wrinkle to frame a kite shape. Overlay within edges of the kite shape toward the outside edges as appeared.

Step 3:
Flip around the paper and blow tenderly beyond all detectable inhibitions end. Your air cushion vehicle should zoom away!

How It Works:

The pocket under the air cushion vehicles trap air and make a zone of high weight. Further, the air moving over the specialty has lower pressure. This distinction makes lift and disposes of the rubbing that typically holds the paper set up on the table. Without grating keeping it down, a little breath is everything necessary to get the air cushion vehicle speeding on its way!

Precautions for Safety:

No precautions! Easy experiment.

Observations:

_____

_____

_____

21. Popping Balloon

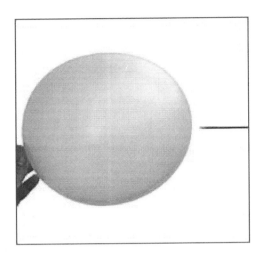

Things You'll Need:

- A Balloon
- A Small Needle
- 2 Pieces of Tape About 2 Inches Each

The Procedure:

Step 1:
Blow the balloon up.
Utilize the two bits of tape to make a "X" on your inflatable.

Step 2:
Cautiously push needle through the center of your "X".

Step 3:
Leave needle in and perceive to what extent it takes your inflatable to pop.

How It Works:

What makes an inflatable pop is called disastrous split spread. This truly entangled sounded state implies that the opening in the inflatable extending is the thing that makes it pop, not the way that air is gradually being let out. At the point when the inflatable's gap gets greater, it tears and inevitably the inflatable pops. In this examination, the tape hinders this procedure.

Precautions for Safety:

Use needle cautiously under adult supervision.

Observations:

_____

_____

_____

22. Expanding Soap

Things You'll Need:

- Soap (Ivory)
- Large Bowl to Put in Microwave

The Procedure:

Step 1:
Spot the bar of cleanser in the bowl, and microwave it on high force for two minutes.

Step 2:

Watch it develop!

Step 3:

Trust that the bowl and froth will cool.

How It Works:

Ivory cleanser has bunches of little air rises in it. As the air bubbles are warmed in the microwave, they get greater. The cleanser is a strong, so once it extends, it remains extended (despite the fact that it contracts a little as it cools)

Precautions for Safety:

Ask some adult to operate the microwave oven for you.

Observations:

_____

_____

_____

23. Dancing Hearts

Utilization of carbonated pop and candy hearts for this trial, to permit the candy to sink, rise, and buoy at various stretches in view of the carbonation.

Things You'll Need:

- A Glass
- Carbonated Pop
- Candy Hearts

The Procedure;
Step 1:

Fill drinking glass with the pop.

Step 2:

Drop all the discussion hearts into the pop.

Step 3:

Watch the hearts move here and there in the pop.

How It Works:

The carbon dioxide gets the sweets hearts and tosses them to the head of the glass. At the point when they arrive at the top, the air pockets burst and the treats works its way down once more.

Precautions for Safety:

Simple experiment having no precautions.

Observations:

_____

_____

_____

24. Weatherman Experiment

Things You'll Need:

- Glass Canning Container
- 4 Ice Cubes
- Plate (Ceramic)
- Hot Water
-

The Procedure:

Step 1:
Pour two creeps of the heated water into the canning container.

Step 2:
Spread the container with the fired plate face up.
Hold up 3 minutes to proceed to the following stage.

Step 3:
Put ice 3D squares on the plate.
Watch your hand crafted water cycle.

How It Works:

What occurs? The virus plate causes the dampness in the warm air, which is inside the container to consolidate and frame water beads. This is something very similar that occurs in the climate. Warm, soggy air rises and meets colder air high in the climate. The water fume gathers and structures precipitation that tumbles to the ground and works its way down once more.

Precautions for Safety:

Don't boil and pour water yourself. Consult some adult.

Observations:

_____

_____

_____

25. Fireworks in Water

Things You'll Need:

- 2 Glasses
- Water
- Fork
- Oil
- Food Coloring

The Procedure:

Step 1:

Fill the tall glass nearly to the top with room-temperature water.
Empty 2 tablespoons of oil into the different glass.

Step 2:

Include 2 drops of food shading to the glass with the oil. Mix the oil into the food shading utilizing a fork. Stop once you break the food shading into littler drops.

Step 3:

Pour the oil and shading blend into the tall glass.
Presently watch! The food shading will gradually soak in the glass, with every bead extending outwards as it falls. It would appear that firecrackers! Isn't that so?

How It Works:

Food shading disintegrates in water, yet not in oil. So when you pour in your food shading/oil blend the oil will glide at the head of the water since it is less thick, and the food shading will begin to break down once they sink through the oil and into the water.

Observations:

_____

_____

_____

26. Blue Tonic Drink

Make a chilled blue drink with tonic water.

Things You'll Need:

- Tonic Water
- Ice
- Black Light
- Citrus Drink
- Glass

The Procedure:

Step 1: Pour carbonated water, citrus drink and ice into a glass.

Step 2:
Turn on black light and sparkle on drink.

Step 3:

Watch it turning in blue!
And then Drink, if you like to.

How It Works:

There is fixing called quinine in carbonated water. It is modest quantities of it, however when it communicates with a dark light it seems blue.

Precautions for Safety:

Avoid watching directly into black light.

Observations:

_____

_____

_____

27. Iconic Egg Drop

Watch an egg dropping due to gravity without breaking.

Things You'll Need:

- Flat Pan
- Drinking Glass
- Water
- Egg
- Cardboard of Toilet Paper Roll
- Ice

The Procedure:

Step 1:
Fill the glass with water and spot a pie skillet straight up on head of the glass.

Step 2:
Spot tissue roll vertically in the center of the pie container.
Balance the egg on head of the bathroom tissue roll so the egg is lying on its side.

Step 3:

When everything is adjusted on head of one another, with one swift and snappy movement hit the side of the pie skillet with your hand. This is an even swing, not a vertical swing. This should be sufficient power to push it off the glass. Watch in excitement as your egg falls into the glass whole without breaking.

How It Works:

It's everything about Inertia! Idleness says an item, the egg for this situation, will remain very still, except if an outside power follows up on it, your hand for this situation. At the point when you move the pie container with your hand, gravity dominates and pulls the egg straight down into the glass of water.

Precautions for Safety:

Perform this experiment in space where you can clean it if it breaks.

Observations:

_____

_____

_____

28. Battling Bubbles

Things You'll Need:

- Vegetable Oil
- Water
- One Aluminum Pan
- 2 Film Canisters and Lids
- 2 Halves of an Alka-Seltzer

The Procedure:

Step 1:
Spot both film canisters in the aluminum container.

Step 2:

Fill one canister to the midpoint with vegetable oil and the other canister with water.

Step 3:

Drop the half of Alka-Seltzer into the vegetable oil canister and top it. At that point do something very similar with the water canister, and step back for wellbeing.
Watch from a protected separation until one of them detonates. Which one was it?

How It Works:

Like the school, a few conditions can be loaded up with energy, different situations can be dull and exhausting. One canister is vivacious and bubbly on account of the compound response that occurs inside the canister and the other is battling for a response.

Precautions for Safety:

Simple experiment.

Observations:

_____

_____

_____

29. Portable Balloon Speakers

Make cheap speakers at home with balloons!

Things You'll Need:

- A Balloon

The Procedure:

Step 1:

Explode the inflatable so it is loaded up with air. Hold the inflatable up to your ear.
Step 2:

Softly tap the opposite side of the inflatable with your finger. Would you be able to hear the sound well? Would you be able to feel the vibrations?

Step 3:

Presently let go of the inflatable. What direction does the air escape? Which course does the inflatable move in?

How It Works:

At the point when you blow into the inflatable you are pushing air atoms into the inflatable. They are constrained into a little territory so are exceptionally near one another. These conditions permit the air particles to convey the sound waves better. That is the reason you can hear the tapping so without any problem. Maybe you constructed a speaker.

Precautions for Safety:

Do not bring the balloon too close to your ears, it can harm your ear drum.

Observations:

_____

_____

_____

30. Polar Beaar Blubber

Things You'll Need:

- 2 Gallon Measured Zipper Lock Packs
- Channel Tape
- Ice (Squashed or in Cubes)
- 1 Gallon Basin
- 4 Tablespoons of Shortening

The Procedure:

Step 1:

Fill basin most of the way with the chilled water. Add enough ice to make water cold.

Step 2:

Include 4 tablespoons of shortening in one of the Ziploc packs. Put void Ziploc pack within the Ziploc sack with shortening in it. Put your hand in the void Ziploc sack, thusly your hand remains clean during the examination. With other hand spread shortening everywhere throughout the outside of the inward pack.

Step 3:

Crease the head of the internal Ziploc pack over the head of the external Ziploc sack. Presently the shortening is stuck between the two sacks. To ensure the shortening remains secure pipe tape this overlay. At last, stick your hand into your new lard glove and plunge it into the container of super cold water.

How It Works:

Shortening is a fat simply as is lard, and fat acts like a protector. A separator prevents vitality from streaming the way that it generally does, from things that are hot to things that are most certainly not. So the body heat that polar bears make is attempting to spill out of the body to the outside cold temperatures, but since of the flubber, it prevents it from getting away.

Observations:

_____

_____

_____

31. Blossoming Beans

Germinating a Pinto Bean at home.

Things You'll Need:

- A Paper Towel
- Pinto Bean
- A Ziploc Bag
- Spray Bottle

The Procedure:

Step 1:

Hose paper towel with splash bottle. Spot wet paper towel in Ziploc Bag. Spot bean on head of wet paper towel.

Step 2:

Close and spot Ziploc Bag in a warm, bright spot.

Step 3:

Add water to paper towel when it dries out. Watch your plant developing in 3-5 days!

How It Works:

What's happening? Germination! That implies the plant is growing its foundations. Marvelous! For the most part, you can't see the roots sprout when the seed is under soil, however since there is no dirt in this testing you can see the entire procedure.

Precautions for Safety:

Simple experiment with no harm.

Observations:

_____

_____

_____

32. Art Surface Tension

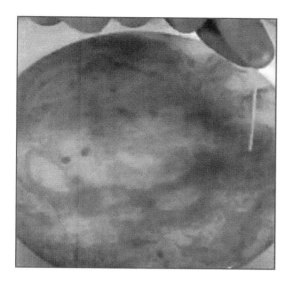

Things You'll Need:

- Straw & Small Paint Brushes
- Acrylic Paints
- Toothpick
- Water
- Dish Soap
- Water Color Paper
- Cups
- Plate

The Procedure:

Step 1:

Spread your work surface with paper towels. In the cups, blend a few paint hues with water in generally equivalent parts. Include a drop of cleanser and a couple of drops of water to another cup.

Step 2:

Pour enough water onto the plate to cover the base. Utilizing the straws, add drops of paint to the outside of the water by plunging a straw into a paint cup at that point delicately contacting the outside of the water with the straw. Utilize a toothpick plunged in cleanser to separate the paint hues and structure designs.

Step 3:

Take a bit of paper sufficiently little to fit on the outside of the water and lay it tenderly in the focal point of the plate. Let it drench for 5-10 seconds, at that point cautiously lift it off and set it onto a paper towel. Utilize another paper towel to delicately wipe the outside of the paper off.

How It Works:

The outside of the water is comprised of a large number of water particles. These little atoms like to be together, and make surface pressure where they meet the air. Surface pressure shields the paint from sinking (for the most part). This is the manner by which water insects remain on the outside of lakes and streams without sinking!

Precautions for Safety:

Best performed under parent's supervision.

Observations:

_____

_____

_____

33. Painted Flowers

Color flowers with your own choice of colors.

Things You'll Need:

- Scissors
- Water
- 3 Plastic Cups
- 3 White Carnations
- Food Coloring (3 Assorted Color Bottles)

The Procedure:

Step 1:

Fill each cup with water midway. Include 3 drops of food shading into every one of the cups. Each cup ought to be an alternate shading.

Step 2:

Painstakingly cut the finish of every one of the blossom's stem. Spot each stem in an alternate shaded water cup.

Step 3:

Hold up one hour and watch your blossoms' petals.
Hold up one day and watch your blossoms' petals.

How It Works:

The Xylem of the bloom works like a lift and brings the water from the cup as far as possible up the plant's stem and into the plant's petals. At the point when it brings the colored water up it winds up kicking the bucket the plant's petals. The Xylem is the thing that permits the plant to get water from the roots right to the petals.

Precautions for Safety:

Use scissors under adult supervision.

Observations:

_____

_____

_____

34. Polished Pennies

You can make your pennies shine with simple experiment.

Things You'll Need;

- Lemon Juice
- Filthy Pennies
- A Cup
- Paper Towels
- Taco Sauce (Optional)

The Procedure:

Step 1:

Put a filthy penny in the cup and spread it with lemon juice.

Step 2:

Hold up around five minutes at that point evacuate the penny and wipe it off with a paper towel.

Step 3:

Attempt the taco sauce to see which works better.

How It Works:

Pennies are made from a metal called copper. The copper blends in with oxygen, similar gas that we relax. This reason something many refer to as oxidation and makes the penny look grimy. Lemon juice has corrosive in it that expels the grimy shading or oxidation and makes the penny quite gleaming once more!

Precautions for Safety:

Do not use so much of taco sauce as it won't work.

Observations:

_____

_____

_____

35. Solar Eclipse Kit

Things You'll Need:

- Scissors
- Shoebox
- Tape
- Toothpick
- Black card
- Yellow Tissue Paper

The Procedure:

Step 1:

Cut a window at each finish of your shoebox and afterward cut a cut over the width (or head) of the case top.

Step 2:

Cut out a square of dark card sufficiently little to slide into the cut in the container. Cut out a hover from the center of the card and stick yellow tissue paper over the gap.

Step 3:

Stick the toothpick to the dark card circle (you will utilize this as your Moon). Slide the square of dark card into the opening on the case and hold the case up to the light. Glance through it to see your Sun.

How It Works:

At the point when you glance through the container's window you will see the case of our sun sparkling splendidly. Be that as it may, when you start to gradually bring down the clear card circle or moon into the residue of the crate, you will gradually observe our sun vanish and make an obscuration. *Note: This trial isn't to be utilized to take a gander at the genuine sun. Taking a gander at the sun can be unsafe.

Precautions for Safety:

Use scissors under adult supervision.

Observations:

_____

_____

_____

36. Homemade Sun Dial

Things You'll Need:

- Bucket
- Sand
- Chalk
- Watch
- 2 Feet Long Stick
- Small Rocks

The Procedure:

Step 1:

Locate a radiant spot and push the stick vertically straight into the grass or earth. On the off chance that your terrace doesn't have any grass or earth, fill a little pail with sand and spot your stick into the can.

Step 2:

Start in the first part of the day when the sun is up. At 7:00 am utilize a little stone or shell to stamp where the shadow of your stick falls. Return at 8:00am, 9:00am, 10:00am, etc until there is no more light in the day. You might need to check your stones with the time they were put utilizing chalk.

Before the day is over your sundial will be finished.

How It Works:

The daylight will make your long stick cast a shadow. The shadow will change it's point depending how the daylight is hitting the stick on the grounds that our earth is continually pivoting and spinning around the sun.

Precautions for Safety:

Make sure you follow on same time.

Observations:

_____

_____

_____

37. Rain Gauge

Things You'll Need:

- Sand
- Scissors
- 2 Liter Plastic Container
- Conduit Tape
- Ruler
- Sharpie Marker

The Procedure:

Step 1:

Void and wash out the 2 liter jug so it's quite spotless. Take the scissors and remove the spout upper right where the shape or bend starts.

Step 2:

Fill base of the container with 1/2 inch of sand. This will shield the jug from falling over on those blustery days. Pour in simply enough water so you can see the water level over the sand. Indeed, your sand will be wet! This is called your immersion point. Utilize the Sharpie Marker to draw a line at the immersion point over the sand. Close to the line express "beginning stage".

Step 3:

Line the ruler up (from the beginning point) and draw a line for each inch up to the head of the container.

Take the top "cut off" ramble segment of the jug and turn it over. Addition it into the container and utilize some channel tape to make sure about it. This part will help catch and gather the precipitation by piping into your jug.

Presently it's an ideal opportunity to locate a decent spot for your downpour measure outside and record your downpour information.

How It Works:

The downpour measure gathers water. At the point when the water dribbles or immerses your downpour check you can precisely quantify how much precipitation has happened.

Precautions for Safety:

Best performed under parent's supervision.

Observations:

_____

_____

38. The Gold Medal

Things You'll Need:

- Toothpicks
- Air Dry Clay
- Circle Cookie Cutter or Mason Jar Lid
- Wax Paper
- Metallic Gold Splash Paint
- Strip
- Little Plastic Blade

The Procedure:

Step 1:

Smooth out delicate dirt. Use Cookie Cutter or Mason Jar Lid to make a round shape into the dirt.
Utilize plastic blade to cut a square shape large enough for the strip to slide through. This should be a fourth of an inch close to one edge of the circle.

Step 2:

 Use toothpicks to draw and create a design onto the clay and let clay dry.
Once dry, use metallic gold spray paint to paint your clay. May need to do two coats. Make sure to do this outside on top of newspaper.

Step 3:

Allow paint to dry. At last, string lace through your award where you cut out the square shape. Tie the lace off and wear it gladly around your neck.

How It Works:

A few solids, similar to dirt beginning off pliable are anything but difficult to twist since they contain water. In any case, when that water dissipates out due to warm, it solidifies and is not, at this point pliable.

Precautions for Safety:

Make sure to have parent supervision while using metallic gold splash paint.

Observations:

_____

_____

_____

39. Vinegar Pops

Things You'll Need:

- Vinegar
- Baking Soda
- Ice Tray
- Food Colors

The Procedure:

Step 1:

Top off ice plate with vinegar. Include food coloring if you wish to do so.

Step 2:

Put ice plate to freeze for four to six hours.

Step 3:

Jump out your Vinegar Pops and plunge them in a plate of preparing pop. Hold up a couple of moments and watch the foaming start.

How It Works:

At the point when you have a corrosive (vinegar) and a base (preparing pop) combined there is a synthetic response. That compound response discharges carbon dioxide and results in the percolating.

Precautions for Safety:

Do not hurry for instant results. Give it some time to form.

Observations:

_____

_____

_____

40. Snow-Flake Making

Things You'll Need:

- White Funnel Cleaners
- Bubbling Water
- String
- Borax
- Wide Mouth Container
- Wooden Pencil

The Procedure:

Step 1:

Take pipe cleaner and cut it into 3 equivalent parts. At that point arrange pipe cleaner parts into a star shape by making a "X" with two of the funnel cleaners and laying the last channel cleaner down the center. Turn pipe cleaners where important to keep them holding together.

Step 2:

Take one finish of a funnel cleaner and append a bit of string to it. At that point connect the opposite finish of the string to the pencil. Cautiously fill the container with the bubbling water. Monitor what number of cups of water you use to fill the container

Step 3:

For some water that is in the container, include three tablespoons of borax. At that point, mix until most or the entirety of the borax has broken down into the water. Put the star into container and let the pencil lay on the edges of the container.
Leave the star for the time being and in the first part of the day you should have a wonderful snowflake to flaunt to your friends and family this Christmas season!

How It Works:

Borax, otherwise called Sodium Borate, breaks up into the warmed water when you mix it. When it cools the water atoms draw nearer together and can't hold as a significant part of the sodium borate, so gems begin to frame to manage the additional borate the water cannot hold anymore.

Precautions for Safety:

Do the entire step 2 under adult supervision.

Observations:

_____

_____

_____

41. Electromagnet Current

Things You'll Need:

- 3 Inches Long Iron Nail
- 3 Inches Long Copper Wire (Thinly Coated)
- Battery
- Paperclips

The Procedure:

Step 1:

Leave around 8 crawls of wire free toward one side and wrap the majority of the remainder of the wire around the nail. Do whatever it takes not to cover the wires.

Step 2:

Cut the wire (if necessary) so that there is about another 8 inches free at the opposite end as well.
Presently expel about an inch of the plastic covering from the two closures of the wire and join the one wire to one finish of a battery and the other wire to the opposite finish of the battery.

Step 3:

Presently you have an Electromagnet! Put the purpose of the nail close to a couple of paper clasps and it should get them!

How It Works:

Most magnets, similar to the ones on numerous fridges, can't be killed, they are called perpetual magnets. Magnets like the one you made that can be turned here and there, are called ELECTROMAGNETS. They run on power and are just attractive when the power is streaming. The power moving through the wire masterminds the particles in the nail with the goal that they are pulled in to specific metals.

Precautions for Safety:

- Try not to overlap the wires.
- Never get the wires of the electromagnet close at family unit outlet! Be protected – have some good times!
- Making an electromagnet goes through the battery to some degree rapidly which is the reason the battery may get warm, so detach the wires when you are finished investigating.

Observations:

_____

_____

_____

42. Homemade Ice Cream

An Easy way to make ice cream a home.

Things You'll Need:

- Half Cup of Milk
- Half Cup of Cream
- Quarter Tablespoon of Chocolate Syrup or the Flavor You Want
- Sugar 4 Tablespoons
- Ice in Huge Quantity
- Half Cup of Rock Salt
- Zip Lock Freezing Bags (Small and Large Both)

The Procedure:

Step 1:

Put the milk, cream, seasoning and sugar into the Small zip-pack and zip it shut. Put about a cup of ice into the big pack and the spread the ice with a little bunch of salt. Put the little sack with your fixings into the bigger pack.

Step 2:

Add some more ice and afterward some increasingly salt. Continue including salt and ice until the sack is practically full. Zip it shut and afterward cautiously hold inverse sides of the sack and shake the pack to and fro for around 5-8 minutes.

Step 3:
Open the bigger pack and take out the littler sack – it ought to be loaded with frozen yogurt. Flush off the pack under running water to evacuate any salt that might be close to the opening of the sack.
Open and appreciate!

How It Works:

At the point when you added salt to the ice, the science between the two constrained the ice to dissolve. Before the ice could dissolve however, it expected to acquire heat from objects that encompass it. This is called an Endothermic procedure. Since your fixings are not as cold as the ice, it obtained heat from your fixings making them colder! At the point when they get colder, they freeze up into frozen yogurt. Yum!

Precautions for Safety:

Be sure the bags are zipped up and closed completely.

Observations:

_____

_____

_____

43. Floating Paper Clip

Things You'll Need:

- Tissue Paper
- Paper Clips
- A Bowl of Water
- Pencil Having an Eraser

The Procedure:

Step 1:
Fill the bowl with water. Attempt to make the paper clip buoy. It won't float.

Step 2:

Tear a bit of tissue paper about a large portion of the size of a dollar note. Tenderly drop the tissue level onto the water.

Step 3:

Tenderly spot a dry paper clip level onto the tissue (do whatever it takes not to contact the water or the tissue)

Utilize the eraser end of the pencil to painstakingly jab the tissue (not the paper clip) until the tissue sinks. The tissue will sink and leave the clip drifting!

How It Works:

How is this conceivable? With a seemingly insignificant detail we researchers call Surface Tension. Fundamentally it implies that there is such a skin on the outside of water where the water atoms hang on close together. On the off chance that the conditions are correct, they can hold sufficiently tight to help your paper cut. The paperclip isn't really skimming; it is being held up by the surface pressure. Numerous creepy crawlies, for example, water striders, utilize this "skin" to stroll over the outside of a stream.

Precautions for Safety:

Make sure you follow the steps precisely for result.

Observations:

_____

_____

_____

44. Swollen Balloons

Things You'll Need:

- Plastic Bottles
- Yeast
- Sugar One Teaspoon
- Balloon
- Warm Water

The Procedure:

Step 1:

Top the jug off with around one inch of warm water. Include the entirety of the yeast bundle and delicately twirl the container a couple of moments.

Step 2:

Include the sugar and whirl it around some more. Like individuals, yeast needs vitality (food) to be dynamic, so we will give it sugar. Presently the yeast is "eating!"

Step 3:

Blow up the inflatable a couple of times to extend it at that point place the neck of the inflatable over the neck of the container. Let the jug sit in a warm spot for around 20 minutes.

On the off chance that all goes well the inflatable will start to swell!

How It Works:

As the yeast eats the sugar, it discharges a gas called carbon dioxide. The gas fills the jug and afterward fills the inflatable as more gas is made. We as a whole realize that there are "gaps" in bread, however how are they made? The appropriate response sounds similar to the plot of a thriller. Most breads are made utilizing Yeast. In all honesty, yeast is really living microorganisms! At the point when bread is made, the yeast gets spread out in flour. Each piece of yeast makes little gas bubbles and that puts a great many air pockets (gaps) in our bread before it gets heated. Naturalist's note – The yeast utilized in this investigation are the related species and strains of Saccharomyces cervisiae. Anyway, when the bread gets prepared in the stove, the yeast kicks the bucket and leaves every one of those air pockets in the bread.

Observations:

_____

_____

_____

45. Blobs in a Bottle

Things You'll Need:

- A Clear Bottle
- 3/4 Cup of Water
- Vegetable Oil
- Bubbling Tablets (Alka Seltzer)
- Food Colors

The Procedure:

Step 1:

Empty the water into the jug. Utilize an estimating cup or channel to gradually empty the vegetable oil into the jug until it's practically full. You may need to sit tight a couple of moments for the oil and water isolation.

Step 2:

Include 10 drops of food coloring to the container. The drops will go through the oil and afterward blend in with the water underneath.

Step 3:

Break a seltzer tablet down the middle and drop the half tablet into the container. Watch it sink to the base and let the blobby significance start. To prop the impact up, simply include another tablet piece. For a genuine astro light impact, sparkle an electric lamp through the base of the jug.

How It Works:

To start, the oil remains over the water on the grounds that the oil is lighter than the water or, all the more explicitly, less thick than water. The oil and water don't blend as a result of something many refer to as "intermolecular extremity." Atomic extremity essentially implies that water particles are pulled in to other water atoms. They get along fine, and can freely bond together (drops.) This is like magnets that are pulled in to one another. Oil particles are pulled in to other oil atoms, they get along fine also. Be that as it may, the structures of the two particles don't permit them to bond together.

At the point when you included the tablet piece, it sank to the base and began dissolving and making a gas. As the gas bubbles rose, they took a portion of the shaded water with them. At the point when the mass of water arrived at the top, the gas got away and down went the water.

Precautions for Safety:

Make sure you follow the steps accordingly.

Observations:

_____

_____

_____

46. Eggshell Crystals

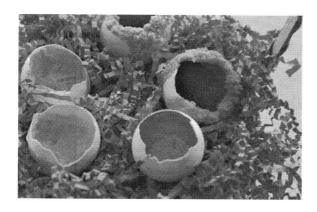

Things You'll Need:

- Clean Eggshells
- Water
- An Assortment of Solvent Solids: (Table salt, Rock Salt, Sugar)
- Little Warmth Verification Holders (Espresso Cups)
- Spoons
- Food Colors
- Egg Containers and Wax Paper or Smaller Than Expected Biscuit Tins

The Procedure:

Step 1:

Split the eggs for this task as near the tight end as could reasonably be expected. This jams more egg to use as a holder for the arrangement. Clean the eggshells utilizing boiling water. The heated water cooks the covering and permits you to pull the skin out of within the egg utilizing your fingers. Try to evacuate all the egg film, if any layer remains inside the shell it is conceivable that your eggshell will develop shape and your gems will turn dark.
Utilize an egg container fixed with waxed paper or smaller than expected biscuit tins to hold the eggs upstanding.

Step 2:

Utilize a pot to warm the water to bubbling. Pour a large portion of a cup to some water into your heatproof compartment. On the off chance that you poured a large portion of some water into the holder, include about a ¼ cup of strong to the water. Mix it until it breaks up. Similarly on the off chance that you utilized some water, include about ½ some strong to the water. You needed to include about half again the volume of the water as a strong to the blend. At the point when the underlying measure of strong is broken up keep including limited quantities of the strong until the water is super-immersed. Super-immersed essentially implies the water has assimilated all it can retain and any strong you include won't break down.

Step 3:

Include food colors. Cautiously empty your answer into the eggshell, filling it as full as conceivable without over-streaming it or making it tip. Locate a protected spot to put your shells while the water dissipates. Precious stones will frame inside the eggshells as the water dissipates.

How It Works:

Dissolving the precious stones in high temperature water made what is known as a "super-immersed arrangement." This fundamentally implies the salts exploited the vitality of the boiling water to assist them with dissolving until there was no more space between atoms in the arrangement. As the arrangement cooled, the water lost its vitality and the precious stones are constrained from the answer for become a strong once more. Since this happens gradually alongside the vanishing, the precious stones have the opportunity to become bigger than they were the point at which the trial began. Common geodes in rock are structure similarly as mineralized water saturates air pockets in rock. This is additionally how rock treats gems are framed.

Precautions for Safety:

Best performed under parent's supervision.

Observations:

_____

_____

_____

47. Plastic Milk

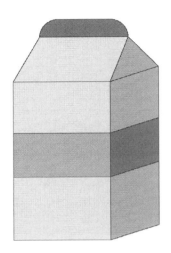

Things You'll Need:

- A Cup of Milk
- Strainer
- White Vinegar
- Bowl

The Procedure:

Step 1:

Request that your amicable grown-up heat up the milk until it is hot, however not bubbling and also ask to deliberately empty the milk into the bowl. Add the vinegar to the milk and work it up with a spoon for about a moment.

Step 2:

Presently the great part, pour the milk through the strainer into the sink. Abandoned in the strainer is a mass of uneven masses.

Step 3:

At the point when it is sufficiently cool, you can flush the masses off in water while you press them together. Presently simply form it into a shape and it will solidify in a couple of days.

How It Works:

You made a substance called Casein. It's from the Latin word signifying "cheddar." Casein happens when the protein in the milk meets the corrosive in the vinegar. The casein in milk doesn't blend in with the corrosive thus it structures masses. Genuine plastics, called polymers, are somewhat unique. On the off chance that you need to make a genuine plastic and get familiar with polymers, attempt the natively constructed Sludge test.

Precautions for Safety:

Ask some adult to handle the boiling and straining part of milk as it will be too hot to handle.

Observations:

_____

_____

_____

48. Chicken Sound

Things You'll Need:

- Cup
- Yarn
- Nail
- Paper Towel

The Procedure:

Step 1:

Cut a bit of yarn around 40 cm long. Request that an elder utilizes the nail to painstakingly punch a hole in the focal point of the base of the cup.

Step 2:

Bind one finish of the yarn to the center of the paper cut. Push the opposite finish of the yarn through the gap in the cup and get it through as appeared in the image. Get a bit of paper towel about the size of a dollar note, at that point overlay it once and get it sodden in the water.

Step 3:

Hold the cup immovably in one hand, and wrap the moist paper towel around the string close to the cup. While you crush the string, pull down in short yanks with the goal that the paper towel firmly slides along the string. On the off chance that all works out in a good way – you will hear a chicken!

How It Works:

This is a case of how a sounding board functions. The vibrations from the string would be practically quiet without the cup, yet when you include the cup, it spreads the vibrations and intensifies them. Pianos and music boxes use wood to go about as a sounding board to make the instrument stronger.

Precautions for Safety:

Best performed under adult supervision.

Observations:

_____

_____

_____

49. The Lincoln High Jump

Things You'll Need:

- Pencil
- A Lincoln Penny (or ther little coin)
- A Bit of Card Stock
- Food Container or Film Canister
- Scissors

The Procedure:

Step 1:

Cut the cardstock paper into a long strip around 75 inches, 2 cm wide and structure it into a loop as appeared. The paper ought to be sufficiently firm to hold the band shape all alone and the circle works best when it is between 8-10 cm over.

Step 2:

For sensational impact, fill the film canister with water and spot on a level surface. Spot the loop on the infant container as appeared and equalization of the penny on the head of the band.

Step 3:

Time for Lincoln's defining moment! Spot a pencil through the focal point of the circle and in one quick movement throw the band out of the way as imagined. In the event that you do this effectively, the circle will fly off the beaten path, and the penny will fall straight down into the container with a sprinkle. 10 focuses for Lincoln…!

How It Works:

Some portion of Newton's first laws says, when all is said in done, that an item very still will stay very still except if followed up on by an outside power. The vitality of your development with the pencil was given to the circle, making it fly off the beaten path rapidly, however the loop moved excessively quick, and there was insufficient grating to influence the penny on head of the band. The penny wound up over the container with nothing to hold it up. It was about then that gravity dominated, and pulled the coin straight down into the holding up water.

Precautions for Safety:

- Take care of the measurements used.
- Do not use scissors alone.

Observations:

_____

_____

_____

50. Changing Color Chemistry

Things You'll Need:

- 3 Clear Plastic Cups
- A 1000 mg Nutrient C Tablet
- Color of Iodine (2%)
- Hydrogen Peroxide (3%)
- Fluid Clothing Starch
- Security Goggles
- Estimating Spoons
- Estimating Cup

The Procedure:

Step 1:

Put on those security goggles and pound the 1000 mg Nutrient C tablet by putting it into a plastic pack and squashing it with a moving pin or the rear of an enormous spoon. Get it into however much of a fine powder as could reasonably be expected. At that point put all the powder in the main cup and include 60 ml of warm water. Mix for in any event 30 seconds. Call this as "Fluid A"

Step 2:

Presently put 1 teaspoon of your fluid into another cup and add to it: 60 ml of warm water and 1 teaspoon of the iodine. Notice the earthy colored iodine turned clear! We should call this "Fluid B." Incidentally, you're finished with Fluid A – you can set it aside.

In the last cup, blend 2 oz of warm water, 1 Tablespoon of the hydrogen peroxide and 1/2 teaspoon of the fluid starch. This is, you gotten it, "Fluid C"

Step 3:

OK, that was a great deal of planning, on to the pleasant part. Assemble the loved ones and empty all of Fluid B into Fluid C. At that point pour them back and forth between the 2 cups a couple of times. Spot the cup down and watch. Show restraint, somewhere close to a couple of moments and a couple of moments, the fluid will out of nowhere turn dull blue!

How It Works:

This is a case of the substance response known as the Iodine clock response. It is known as a clock response since you can change the sum if time it takes for the fluids to turn blue. The science of the exhibit gets somewhat muddled, however essentially it is a clash of science between the starch which is attempting to turn the iodine blue, and the Nutrient C which is shielding it from turning blue. In the long run the Nutrient C loses and, bam! You get moment blueness.

Precautions for Safety:

- This investigation should just be finished with the assistance of a grown-up. Iodine will recolor pretty much anything it contacts and it very well may be dangerous. Hydrogen peroxide can cause eye and skin disturbance – security goggles are required all through the investigation. Be certain your accommodating grown-up peruses the alert names on every holder.

- Cautiously dump all fluids with a lot of water and wash your hands. Reuse the cups or discard them in the refuse.

Observations:

_____

_____

_____

51. Changing Color Chemistry

Things You'll Need:

- 1 Liter Plastic Soft Drink Container with a Cap
- A Ball Point Pen Top That Doesn't Have Gaps in it
- Modeling Clay

The Procedure:

Step 1:

Expel any marks from your jug with the goal that you can watch the activity. Fill the container to the top with water.   Spot a little pea-size bit of demonstrating dirt toward the finish of the point on the pen top.

Step 2:

Gradually place the pen top into the jug, demonstrating earth end first. It should scarcely skim. On the off chance that it sinks remove some mud. In the event that it glides a lot of include more earth. Presently screw on the jug top overall quite close.

Step 3:

Presently for the pleasant part. You can make the pen top ascent and fall at your order. Press the container hard – the pen top sinks - quit crushing and the pen top ascents. With a little practice, you can even get it to stop directly in the center.

How It Works:

This experiment is about thickness. At the point when you press the jug, the air bubble in the pen top gets littler and that makes it thicker than the water around it. At the point when this occurs, the pen sinks. At the point when you quit pressing, the air pocket gets greater once more, the water is constrained out of the top, and the pen top ascents.
On the off chance that it doesn't work: mess with the measure of dirt and be certain the jug is filled to the top before putting on the cap.

Precautions for Safety:

Do follow step after step carefully for getting the best of results.

Observations:

_____

_____

_____

52. Rolling a Can

Things You'll Need:

- An Empty Can
- Blown up balloon
- A Head of Hair

The Procedure:

Step 1:

Spot the can on its side on a level smooth surface like a table or a smooth floor.

Step 2:

Rub the blown balloon to and fro through your hair truly quick.

Step 3:

Hold the balloon the can without really contacting the can. The can will begin to move towards the balloon without you in any event, contacting it!

How It Works:

At the point when you rub the inflatable through your hair, imperceptible electrons (with a negative charge) develop on the outside of the inflatable. This is called friction based electricity, which signifies "immobile power" The electrons have the ability to pull positive charge toward them – like the soft drink can.

Precautions for Safety:

Simple fun experiment!

Observations:

_____

_____

_____

53. Tissue Apparition

Things you will need;

- A Piece of Tissue Paper
- A Balloon
- Scissors
- A Head of Hair
- Spooky Music (optional)

The Procedure:

Step 1:

First cut out an apparition shape in the tissue as appeared about 4 cm long and make eyes with a marker. In the event that you are utilizing 2-handle tissues, strip separated the 2 layers to get the tissue as dainty as could be expected under the circumstances. Cut out a couple of phantoms for increasingly fun and spot them on a level surface. You should make some out of normal paper to look at.

Step 2:

Blow the balloon and tie it. At that point rub it truly quick through your hair for around 10 seconds. This will include a static charge.

Step 3:

Gradually bring the balloon close to the apparition, and the phantom will start to ascend towards it. If the inflatable is sufficiently charged, the phantom will rise and buoy straight up to the inflatable, in any event, when it is a few inches away. With a little practice, you can get the apparition to rise, drift, and even move around.

How It Works:

At the point when you rub the inflatable through your hair, undetectable electrons with a negative charge develop on the outside of the inflatable. The electrons have the ability to pull exceptionally light items with a positive charge toward them – for this situation, the tissue apparition!

Precautions for Safety:

The most effortless approach to make the apparition ascend without it adhering to the inflatable is to tape the very tip of the base of the phantom to a table. The apparition will rise and move alongside the inflatable. With a decent charge, the inflatable can control the phantom from a few inches away.

Observations:

_____

_____

_____

54. Hoop Glider

Things You'll Need:

- Tape
- Scissors
- 3X5 Inch Hard Paper
- Plastic Straw

The Procedure:

Step 1:

Cut the list card or solid paper into 3 separate pieces that measure 2.5 cm by 13 cm. Take 2 of the bits of paper and tape them together into a band as appeared. Make certain to cover the pieces about a large portion of 1 cm with the goal that they keep a pleasant round shape once taped.

Step 2:

Utilize the last segment of paper to make a little loop, covering the edges somewhat like previously.
Tape the paper circles to the finishes of the straw as demonstrated as follows. (Notice that the straw is arranged within the circles)

Step 3:

Presently hold the straw in the center with the bands on top and toss it noticeable all around like how you may toss a dart calculated marginally up. With some training you can get it to go farther than many paper planes.

How It Works:

It might look unusual, yet you will find it flies shockingly well. The two sizes of loops help to keep the straw adjusted as it flies. The huge loop makes "drag" (or air opposition) which helps keep the straw level while the little circle in at the front keeps your super Hooper from killing course. Some have inquired as to why the plane doesn't turn over since the bands are heavier than the straw. Since objects of various weights by and large fall at a similar speed, the band will keep its "upstanding" position.

Precautions for Safety:

Fun and simple experiment.

Observations:

55. Frozen Slime

Things You'll Need:

- Glitter Glue
- Borax 1 Teaspoon
- Water Half Cup
- Glass Container

The Procedure:

Step 1:

Empty the bottle of glitter glue in glass container and put some water in which it becomes a paste.

Step 2:

Put a teaspoon of borax in half cup of warm water.

Step 3:

Add the borax water in glue water and mix well.
Wait for the magic!

How It Works:

Paste contains a fixing called polyvinyl acetic acid derivation, which is a fluid polymer. Borax helps the polymer strands stay together, making sludge.

Precautions for Safety:

Borax part should be handled under adult supervision.

Observations:

_____

_____

_____

56. Invisible Note

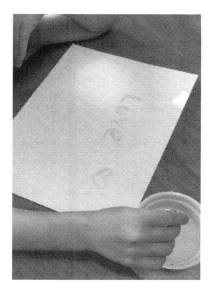

Things You'll Need:

- Bowl
- Cotton Bud
- Lemon Juice
- Hair Dryer
- White Paper

The Procedure:

Step 1:

Pour the lemon juice in to a bowl.

Step 2:

Dip the cotton bud in it and write your secret note on the white construction paper.

Step 3:

Let it dry. After drying use a hair dryer with less warm air to blow it on the paper.

You'll see the hidden note appear on it.

How It Works:

At the point when you heat up the lemon juice, it disintegrates and discharges carbon. When the carbon contacts the air, it oxidizes and permits you to see the message when you hold it up to the light! Undetectable ink uncovers mystery message.

Precautions for Safety:

Use the hair dryer with an adult's help.

Observations:

_____

_____

_____

57. Edible Chocolate Slime

Things You'll Need:

- 14 oz Sweetened Condensed Milk Can
- Corn Starch 1/3 Cup
- Chocolate Bar

The Procedure:

Step 1:

Mix all the ingredients in a pan and put it on the flame.

Step 2:

Mix until they make a uniform mixture.
Add a little cornstarch to make the mixture lose a bit of stickiness.

Step 3:

Let it cool a bit and then use it as a slime!

How It Works:

Cornstarch will help the mixture in binding together making perfect slime. Now stretch, play and then eat later on if it's in the condition to eat.

Precautions for Safety:

- Make sure not to use too much cornstarch.
- Do the procedure under parent's supervision.

Observations:

_____

_____

_____

58. Balloon in a Bottle

Things you will need;
-   Balloon
-   A Narrow Necked Bottle
-   Water 1-2 tablespoons

The Procedure:

Step 1:

Add 2 tablespoons of water in a bottle. Now put the bottle in microwave for about 1 minute so that it will boil.

Step 2:

Stretch the opening of balloon over the neck of the bottle and sit back to wait.

Step 3:

Right after 30 seconds gradually the ends of the balloon will start moving inside the bottle and finally it will start to expand inside it.

How It Works:

Since the pressure is higher outside, air hurries into the bottle taking the inflatable alongside it. The more the container chills off, the more air rolls in all things considered, and the more the inflatable grows inside the bottle.

Precautions for Safety:

Ask some adult to handle the bottle after putting it inside the oven as it will be too hot.

Observations:

_____

_____

_____

59. Vanishing Egg Shell

Things You'll Need:

- An Egg
- White Vinegar
- Glass

The Procedure:

Step 1:

Pour white vinegar in water as much so that the egg gets immersed in it.

Step 2:

Dip egg into it. In a few minutes you will see bubbles in the vinegar.

Step 3:

Leave it for a week and then observe. After a week you'll see the eggshell will disappear.

How It Works:

Eggshells are comprised of calcium carbonate, which effectively responds with the corrosive in vinegar called acidic corrosive. The calcium carbonate is broken by acidic corrosive and along these lines, the eggshell is disintegrated.

Precautions for Safety:

Do not try to drink vinegar.

Observations:

_____

_____

_____

60. Tornado Inside a Bottle

Things You'll Need:

- A Bottle
- Some Water
- Glitter
- Few Drops of Dish Washing Liquid

The Procedure:

Step 1:

Fill around 70 % water in a bottle.

Step 2:

Add few drops of dishwashing liquid and glitter into it.

Step 3:

Turn the bottle upside down and hold the bottle's neck. Now move it in circular motion for viewing the tornado.

How It Works:

At the point when we turn the bottle in the round movement, it makes a water vortex. At that point the water starts to quickly turn around the vortex on account of centripetal power which is an internal power that coordinates an article or liquid, for example, water towards the focal point of its round way.

Observations:

_____

_____

_____

61. Magic Expanding Balloon

Things You'll Need:

- A Balloon
- A Bottle
- Vinegar
- Baking Soda

The Procedure:

Step 1:

Fill around 33% of vinegar inside the bottle.

Step 2:

Add 2 tablespoons of baking soda inside the balloon.

Step 3:

Cover the neck of the bottle with the opening of balloon and then lift the balloon so that the baking soda is dropped into it. As soon as the soda is dropped into the bottle, the balloon will inflate.

How It Works:

This is the least complex response between a corrosive and a base. At the point when they're blended they make a substance response that outcome in the development of carbon dioxide gas. The particles of the gases move at a rapid every which way. As the carbon dioxide tops off in the bottle, it has no place to go so it starts to fill the inflatable.

Precautions for Safety:

Be careful with handling the ingredients.

Observations:

---

62. Rocket Balloon

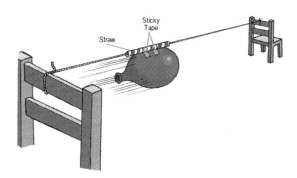

Things You'll Need:

- Balloon
- Straw
- Sticky Tape
- Rope
- Two Chairs

The Procedure:

Step 1:

Attach one end of the string with some support such as a chair. Pass the other end from a straw and attach it with some other support.

Step 2:

Blow up a balloon but do not tie it up. Now with the help of sticky tape attach the balloon with the straw.

Step 3:

Keeping the balloon and straw thing to one end of the string leave the balloon and watch it fly as a rocket!

How It Works:

This entire analysis is about thrust and air. As the air surges out of the inflatable it makes the inflatable travel forward called push. Push is the pushing power made by vitality. In this test, this vitality is delivered by the air coming out of the inflatable.

Precautions for Safety:

Best performed with adults' help.

Observations:

_____

_____

_____

63. Parachute Experiment

Things You'll Need:

- A Plastic Bag
- Strings
- Some Weight (Glass or Anything Like That)

The Procedure:

Step 1:

Cut a large plastic bag into the shape of an octagon having (8 sides). Make a small hole at each corner.

Step 2:

Put the strings in all the corners and attach them all with some weight such as glass.

Step 3:

Now drop it from some high point as slow as possible. And observe how well it works!

How It Works:

Your parachute will plummet gradually to the ground, giving your weight a happy landing. At the point when you discharge the parachute the weight pulls down on the strings and opens up a huge surface zone of material that utilizes air hindrance to slow it down. The bigger the surface region the more air obstruction and the more slowly the parachute will drop.

Precautions for Safety:

While dropping it from high spot consult some adult.

Observations:

_____

_____

_____

64. Potato Lightbulb

Things You'll Need:

- Potato
- 1-Volt LED Bulb
- Wire
- Needle
- 2 Nails (one of zinc and the other of copper)

The Procedure:

Step 1:

Put both the nails in a potato around 1 cm apart from each other.

Step 2:

Take a copper wire and remove the plastic from it. Attach each wire with each nail.

Step 3:

Attach other ends of the wires with a LED bulb. After sometime you'll observe light in the bulb.

How It Works:

The science behind this is quite basic. A potato contains sugar, water and corrosive. Explicit sorts of metals – particularly copper and zinc – react with the potato when they are plunged inside. The metals productively become cathode, one positive and the other negative, and electrons begin to stream in a stream between the metals inside the potato, making somewhat electric flow.

Precautions for Safety:

Be careful while handling the nails and wires.

Observations:

_____

_____

_____

65. Coke Volcano

Things You'll Need:

- A 2 Litre Diet Coke
- 2 Packs of Mentos Mints
- Tape
- Piece of Paper

The Procedure:

Step 1:

Open the bottle cap and place it on a flat surface.

Step 2:

Roll the paper in the shape of a tube, put one finger at one end of the tube and from the other end start adding Mentos into it.

Step 3:

Bring it near the mouth of the bottle and drop the Mentos into it. You'll see an amazing coke volcano.

How It Works:

The explanation for this is the synthetics in the Mentos respond with the Diet Coke to cause loads of carbon dioxide air pockets to shape on the outside of the mints rapidly. This develops a great deal of weight in the jug and that causes a fantastic fly of air pockets shooting into the air.

Precautions for Safety:

Do not drink coke over mentos.

Observations:

_____

_____

_____

66. Hot Ice Tower

Things You'll Need:

- Vinegar 4 Cups
- Baking Soda 4 Tablespoons
- Container

The Procedure:

Step 1:

Put 4 cups of vinegar in a container and gradually add 4 tablespoons of baking soda in it.

Step 2:

Heat the mixture until it remains 3/4 cups and then refrigerate it for 40 -45 minutes.

Step 3:

After taking it out pour it in a container very slowly so that it crystallizes. You'll observe a tower.

How It Works:

The sodium acetic acid derivation blend contains water. We diminished the proportion of water in the blend by warming it, be that as it may, there is still water in there. The water particles shield the sodium acetic acid derivation blend from encircling precious stones. Taking everything into account, gems may start to shape, however as two or three particles join, the water iotas pull them isolated again. Right when we cooled the blend, we had the choice to bring the sodium acetic acid derivation blend down to a temperature lower than where it would normally go into a strong. Thusly it was super-cooled. The crystallization procedure radiates heat since it is an exothermic response. So the hot ice is hot to the touch.

Precautions for Safety:

If you don't add baking soda slowly then you'll get vinegar and baking soda volcano which would overflow your container.

Observations:

_____

_____

_____

67. 7-Layer Density Column

LAMP OIL
RUBBING ALCOHOL
VEGETABLE OIL
WATER
DISH SOAP
MILK
100% MAPLE SYRUP
CORN SYRUP
HONEY

Things You'll Need:

- Dish Washing Soap
- Milk
- Vegetable Oil
- Lamp Oil
- Honey
- Liquid
- Corn Syrup
- Water
- Rubbing Alcohol

The Procedure:

Step 1:

Add the fluids one by one in such a way that the heaviest is at bottom.

Step 2:

Add honey at very first in a way that it doesn't stick to the walls.

Step 3:

Then add all other fluids one by one so that the lightest is on top. You may skip few if they are not available.

How It Works;

The heaviest liquid has the most mass per unit volume or the most significant thickness. A bit of the liquids doesn't stir up since they shock each other (oil and water). Various liquids restrict blending since they are thick and gooey.

Precautions for Safety:

Easy experiment to perform!

Observations:

_____

_____

_____

68. Colorful Volcano

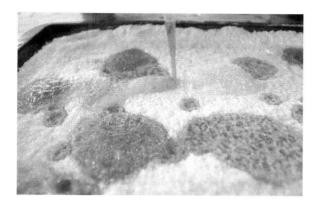

Things You'll Need:

- Food Colors or Any
- Baking Soda
- Lemon Juice
- Tray

The Procedure:

Step 1:

Add lemon juice in a tray and dilute it by adding some vinegar.

Step 2:

Then add different colors randomly in portions.

Step 3:

Now sprinkle baking soda on it to see the colorful volcano.

How It Works:

This examination is fundamentally a corrosive base response. At the point when corrosive from lemon, citrus extract responds with base (heating pop) two new synthetic substances are shaped, carbonic corrosive and sodium acetic acid derivation. The new acids at that point deteriorate into water and carbon dioxide is created which causes bubbles. The blend ejects like a well of lava in view of the blending of lemon juice and the heating pop.

Precautions for Safety:

Do not taste anything.

Observations:

_____

_____

_____

69. Leaf Rubbing

Things You'll Need:

- Wax Paper or Tracing Paper
- Oil Paints, Crayons or Pencil Colors
- Leaves of Different Sizes and Shapes
- Clipboard or Any Hard Surface

The Procedure:

Step 1:

Take a leaf on a clipboard and place the paper on it.

Step 2:

Now carefully without moving the paper, rub the crayons or colors on it so that the leaf is traced.

Step 3:

Repeat the same with all types of leaves and colors to get wonderful designs.

How It Works:

This activity will help the kids to discover different parts of its leaves and the veins of leaves will make beautiful designs.

Precautions for Safety:

Best performed under adult supervision.

Observations:

_____

_____

_____

70. Air Vortex Cannon

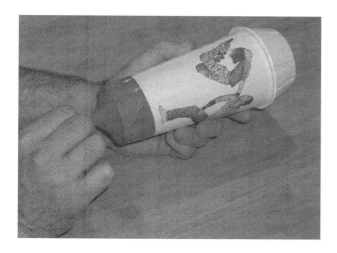

Things You'll Need:

- Plastic Cup
- Balloon
- Rubber Band
- Scissors

The Procedure:

Step 1:

Cut the round hole in the bottom of the cup then blow up a balloon completely to stretch it out and let the air out. Cut the neck of the balloon with scissors.

Step 2:

Stretch the balloon to the upper opening of the paper cup and overlap the remaining cover completely. Use rubber band to wrap the balloon from upper side of the cup.

Step 3:

Hold the lower side of the cup in one hand and stretch the balloon from centre with one hand and pull the balloon back to fire it.

How It Works:

This air vortex gun works just by applying power rapidly and effectively to air atoms. As air particles are in a semi-closed cup, they have just one opening. So when we stretch the balloon and discharge it, it pushes the air particles in forward position. These particles apply power on different atoms and a chain of response of rapid impacts is created. The main path for these air particles to escape is through the main opening in the base. So the air can be take shots at certain items.

Precautions for Safety:

- Be careful while cutting the base hole, you might cut your finger.
- Use rubber bands gently while wrapping around the balloon.

Observations:

_____

_____

_____

71. Magical Crystals

Things You'll Need:

- Refined Water
- Salt
- Wire
- Glass Jar or Container

The Procedure:

Step 1:

Boil the water till bubbles appears. Fill the half container with hot water.

Step 2:

Take good quantity of salt and mix it well.

Step 3:

Place the loop of wire in the container and place the container in warm place. You will see crystals around wire in couple of days.

How It Works:

This experiment works given the temperature change of the water, and the ability to be dissoluble, of the salt. As the water cools, the solvency of the salt in the mix reduces, and the salt urges onto the wire to shape precious crystals.

Precautions for Safety:

Be careful while handling boiling water.

Observations:

_____

_____

_____

72. The Water Refraction

Things You'll Need:

- Glass Container
- Water
- Pen or Marker
- Paper

The Procedure:

Step 1:

Fill the half container.

Step 2:

Draw an arrow on the paper using maker or pen.

Step 3:

Place the paper behind the container and you will see the refraction.

How It Works:

Refraction happens when the light goes between two mediums. In the refraction, the light goes from the air, through the glass, the water, the glass once more, and air again before showing up at your eyes. The light that was at the tip of the arrow is currently on the correct side and the light on the correct side is presently on the left concerned.

Precautions for Safety:

Handle the glass container carefully.

Observations:

_____

_____

_____

73. Home Made Projector

Things You'll Need:

- Cardboard Box
- Smartphone
- Magnifying Glass
- Marker
- Knife
-

The Procedure:

Step 1:

Pick a rectangular shoe box, and hold the magnifying glass to the short side in the middle and follow around the focal point of the magnifying glass with the assistance of a marker.

Step 2:

Cut out this followed circle by utilizing a blade or a sharp scissor. Cut it as smoothly as you can.

Step 3:

Append your magnifying glass to the opening you cut before and fix it there. That is it. Test your magnifying glass by setting your mobile phone up-side-down against the magnifying glass and play the video. Close the box by putting a book over it or taping its opening, to make it as dim as could reasonably be expected. Point the box at a white wall in a dull room, sit back, and relax!!

How It Works:

A magnifying glass is a convex lens, it is used to produce a magnified image of the object and we know that it also produces an upside down image of the object but the wall cannot flip the image that's why the phone is placed upside down in the box. The magnifying glass enlarges this image and projects it on your wall/screen.

Precautions for Safety:

Be careful while cutting the hole for magnifying glass with knife.

Observations:

_____

_____

_____

74. Glowing Water Bottle

Things You'll Need:

- 3 Bottles
- 3 Highlighters
- Tonic Water
- Tap Water
- Black Light

The Procedure:

Step 1:

Prepare the water with the first bottle, make it, pull back a simple scar and throw the indicator ink into the bottle.

Step 2:

Simply fill the bottle with tap water and set aside. Select the first bottle and add water to the illustrator ink and stir it to mix well. Repeat the same steps for all the remaining bottles.

Step 3: Now that all three bottles are ready and in the right order. Put a black light on the back of these three bottles and open them. Bottles of tonic water and Highlight ink will start to burn.

How It Works:

A bottle of light tap water does not light up because it was empty. While the water-tone bottles and mirror ink began to burn because they both had the same chemical in it known as quinine containing phosphorus. Great light in our work, this UV light is provided by dark light and the phosphorous molecules are excited and begin to emit light.

Precautions for Safety:

Wear gloves to avoid contact with high lighter in.

Observations:

_____

_____

_____

75. Power of Sunlight

Things you will need;

- Pizza Box
- Transparent Foil
- Foil
- Stick
- Tape
- Scissors

The Procedure:

Step 1:

Open the lid of the pizza box and cut a square around ¾ of the size. Cut the foil of same size as of square and attach it under the square face.

Step 2:

lift the square up and wrap the transparent sheet around the lid properly so no air can enter. Use tape to stick the transparent foil properly.

Step 3:

lift the lid and place the food which you want to heat and close the lid. Lift the square with foil and place it in the direction of sun. Use stick to hold the square upward. Wait for a while till sun plays the magic and warms up your food.

How It Works:

This experiment relies on temperature of the day, the time and intensity of the daylight. These all are exceptionally fundamental for your sun oriented stove to work as indicated by our arrangement. The daylight conveys the vitality to the crate/box and afterward this vitality or warmth is caught inside the case which warms our food when set inside.

Precautions for Safety:

Be careful while cutting the square.

Observations:

_____

_____

_____

76. Levitating Paper

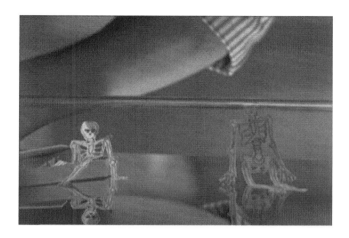

Things You'll Need:

- Paper
- Wool
G- lass Rod

The Procedure:

Step 1:

Cut the paper into small pieces or the shapes you want to pull.

Step 2:

Rub the glass rod against the wool for few minutes.

Step 3:

Place the rod close to the paper and boom your paper will start to get attached with the rod.

How It Works:

The sort of power you just created by scouring is known as electricity produced via friction. The delicate wool rubs a portion of the electrons from the outside of the glass pole, making a positive charge. At the point when you carry the glass bar to the paper piece it pulls in them in view of charge.

Precautions for Safety:

Try not to touch the side of glass you are rubbing against the wool.

Observations:

_____

_____

_____

77. Balloon Powered Car

Things You'll Need:

- Lego and Lego Wheels
- Balloon

The Procedure:

Step 1:

Use Lego to build the car of your desired shape and attach Lego wheels to it.

Step 2:

Make a hole in the spoiler of the car to attach the balloon.

Step 3:

Blow up the balloon and put it inside the hole of spoiler so and leave the end of the balloon. Your car will rush forward by the air pressure. You can try different variants like change the size of balloon and weight of the car to see different effects of air pressure and weight.

How It Works:

This is application of Newton law of motion which states" Body will stay stationery until a force acts on it". The car will not move until you leave the back hole of balloon. The air pressure makes the car go forward.

Observations:

_____

_____

_____

78. Magical Corn

Things You'll Need:

- Clean Jar
- Popping Corn
- 3 Cups Water
- 2 Tablespoon Baking Soda
- 6 Tablespoon Vinegar
- Food Colors
-

The Procedure:

Step 1:

Fill the jar with water and add few drops of food color to it. Then add some baking soda and mix it until it is completely dissolved.

Step 2:

Add a small quantity of popping corn into the water.

Step 3:
Add vinegar to the jar and watch these corns hop up and down for an hour.

How It Works:

When the baking soda and vinegar are combined, they respond and structure carbon dioxide gas. Carbon dioxide gas produces rises in the water which hover around the corn. Gas atoms being less thick than water so they move upward to escape through the container, these air pockets lift the corn along them. At the point when the air pocket arrives at the surface it pops and the corn goes to the base once more. This jumping will proceed until the response among vinegar and baking drink is finished.

Precautions for Safety:

Maintain the distance form jar while performing the experiment. Wash your hands before touching your eyes.

Observations:

_____

_____

_____

79. Home Made Electroscope

Things You'll Need:

- Glass Jar of Medium Height with a Lid
- Tape
- Copper Wire
- Scissors
- Aluminum Foil
- Piece of Wool or Balloon
- Straw
-

The Procedure:

Step 1:

Use scissors to cut the straw about two inches long. Make a hole in the lid so that straw can pass. Insert your straw in the hole and fix it on the jar using glue or tape.

Step 2:

Cut a 10-inch piece of metal. Make a string of threads around the first 4 inches. Bind the straight edge of the fence with grass and create a link about 1 inch.

Step 3:

Hang two pieces of foil in this hook. Make sure they are in touch. After this, Place the metal end in the pot and twist or touch the lid on the pot. Now call out your individual items, bringing them closer to the wire attached to your electroscope.

How It Works:

An electroscope is an early logical instrument which is used to detect the presence of electric charge on a body.
Precautions for your safety;
Be careful with wires since they are sharp do not get your hands priced

Observations:

_____

_____

_____

80. Sense of Sounds

Things You'll Need:

- Pencil
- Rubber Bands
- Cardboard Rolls or Tubes
- Wax Paper
- Color Paints

The Procedure

Step 1:

Take a wax paper and cover one end of the cardboard roll/tube by using a rubber band.

Step 2:

Make a hole in the side of tube and color it for decoration purpose.

Step 3:

Now by using the other open end of the tube make sound. You'll observe different sounds from different rolls.

How It Works:

As you sing, talk or murmur beyond all detectable inhibitions end, your vocal strings make sound waves that movement through the instrument. At the point when the sound waves travel through the cylinder, a portion of the sound waves ricochet off the dividers of the instrument. This adjustment in heading can add music to the sound of the voice.

Precautions for Safety:

Be careful when making hole in the tube.

Observations:

_____

_____

_____

81. Flip A Glass

Things You'll Need:

- Cardboard
- Glass Filled with Water

The Procedure:

Step 1:

Put the cardboard over the mouth of the glass, ensuring that no air bubbles enter the glass as you grip the cardboard.

Step 2:

Flip around the glass. Evacuate your hand which was holding the cardboard. The cardboard and water should stay same.

How It Works:

With no air inside the glass, the gaseous tension from outside the glass is more critical than the weight of the water inside the glass. The extra pneumatic stress makes sense of how to hold the cardboard set up, keeping you dry and your water where it should be, inside the glass.

Precautions for Safety:

Make sure to handle the glass carefully.

Observations:

_____

_____

_____

82. Slipping of Egg

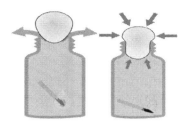

Things You'll Need:

- An Egg
- A Match Stick
- A Jar

The Procedure:

Step 1:

Put a boiled egg on the neck of the jar it won't go down.

Step 2:

Now add a light up match stick inside the jar and then place the egg over jar's neck.

Step 3:

After sometime you'll notice the egg will slip down the neck.

How It Works:

At the point when you include the match, you cause the air inside to extend, this will push the egg up marginally and some air will get away. As the air by then chills off again it starts to recoil, this pulls the egg down and outlines a nice seal. This implies the pneumatic stress inside the jug will diminish permitting the gaseous tension outside to drive the egg into the jug. Furthermore, in light of the fact that a bubbled egg is exceptionally rubbery and adaptable you can get it into a container that has a neck far littler than you would anticipate.

Precautions for Safety:

Be careful while handling the match stick.

Observations:

83. Water Xylophone

Things You'll Need:

- Food Shading
- Water
- Wooden Sticks
- 4+ Artisan Containers

The Procedure:

Step 1:

To begin, fill the containers with shifting degrees of water. You can eyeball the sums or get the estimating cups and get somewhat more logical with your investigation.

Step 2:

More water approaches lower sound or pitch and less water rises to a higher sound or pitch. You would then be able to add food shading to make various hues for each note.

How It Works:

Sound waves are vibrations that movement through the medium which for this situation is water. At the point when you change the measure of water in the containers or glasses, you likewise change the sound waves.

Precautions for Safety:

Easy fun experiment.

Observations:

_____

_____

_____

84. Homemade Hovercraft

Things You'll Need:

- CD
- Balloon
- Bottle Cap

The Procedure:

Step 1:

Make a hole in the cap of water bottle.

Step 2:

Fix the balloon over the water bottle using glue.

Step 3:

Stick the cap over the CD and blow the balloon. When your are ready give this hover a push and see it gliding over the table.

How It Works:

Genuine Hovercrafts takes a shot at a similar guideline, the air discharge from the balloon and makes a pad of air between the CD, and surface this diminishes the rubbing between the cd and the surface yet this will keep on working just until the balloon is loaded up with air.

Observations:

---

85. Green Slime

Things You'll Need:

- Bowl
- Corn Flour
- Water
- Food Coloring

The Procedure:

Step 1:

Take a bowl and mix water and corn flour in it. Mix it till it becomes a thick paste.

Step 2:

Now add few drops of food coloring to it.

Step 3:

Then stir your mixture slowly and then increase the speed gradually. Your slime is ready and feels like rock.

How It Works:

Corn flour slime is a case of a shear-thickening fluid. Corn flour slime is an alternate kind of fluid. It doesn't observe the regular guidelines and properties of liquid. At the point when weight is applied on slime, its strength increases and the slime get thicker. Sooner or later, the slime may begin to lose it liquid like shape and act more as strong. In spite of the fact that there are many shear-thickening liquids nobody precisely comprehends why they carry on such properties.

Precautions for Safety:

Don't use hands to mix the slime.

Observations:

_____

_____

_____

86. Colored Fire

Things You'll Need:

- Glass Jars
- Fuels
- Colorant

The Procedure:

Step 1:

Set all the chemicals separately. You will need only half tablespoon of chemicals. Use methanol for vivid coloring of fire.

Step 2:

Take some chemical put it in jar and add some fuel in it, then light it up from any end.

Step 3:

To change the color of fire you have to change the fuel like for blue fire use alcohol from sanitizers, for green fire use boric acid which is found in insect killer, for orange fire you will need bleaching powder and for red fire you will need lithium salt from lithium battery.

How It Works:

This technique is used in fir works, you see fire of different colors red , green, blue etc. when we add different chemicals with fuel to burn they result in different atomic spectra which adds different colors to fire.

Precautions for Safety:

Be careful while playing with fire. Try to sit away while lighting up the fire.

Observations:

_____

_____

_____

87. Rubber Band Car

Things You'll Need:

- Tape
- Scissors
- Ice Cream sticks
- Rubber Bands
- 4 Bottle Caps

The Procedure:

Step 1:

Sharpen the ends of ice cream sticks so that they could pass the bottle caps.

Step 2:

Make gaps in bottle tops and join the two sticks with two, two individually. Secure outside of the wheel with glue. At that point join these two front and back wheels to stay with one another.
Structuring and innovativeness are for the most part yours you can make the body by joining sticks.

Step 3:

At that point fix a little bit of a toothpick in the front stick, size ought to be less so it can turn unreservedly without hitting the ground. Connect an elastic band to the back axle. Associate elastic band circle to the front toothpick, bend to twist up, and release.

How It Works:

The elastic bands can be extended, and they store potential vitality when they're extended. The versatile potential vitality is put away which is a direct result of the distortion capacity of the elastic band without breaking until a specific point. At the point when you discharge the extended elastic band all the put away vitality needs to head off to some place, more often than not it is changed over into motor vitality. In our model, we utilized this put away vitality to gracefully motor vitality to our vehicle to move when we append an elastic band with an axle and a wheel.

Precautions for Safety:

Be careful while making holes in the bottle caps.

Observations:

---

88. Bridge Construction

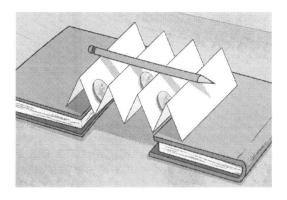

Things You'll Need:

- 2 Books
- Pennies
- Paper Strip

The Procedure:

Step 1:

Put the paper strip over and between two books and place few pennies on it. The bridge will collapse.

Step 2:

Now fold the paper multiple times like for making an airplane.

Step 3:

Put multiple pennies in its different folds. Now the bridge won't collapse.

How It Works:

This little designing movement will get kids considering the reasons why different structures are manufactured the manner in which they are. As you noticed, the paper with collapsing had the option to clutch more weight than the typical one is on the grounds that the paper is powerless under pressure and is to some degree solid under strain. So when we overlay or roll the paper, it builds the thickness of paper, which permits the paper to fortify itself.

Observations:

_____

_____

_____

89. Straw Rocket

Things You'll Need:

- Paper
- Straw

The Procedure:

Step 1:

Cut a square shape paper to make the body of the rocket. Wrap this paper length-wise around a paper and stick it through the tape to make a shut cylinder.

Step 2:

Line up the square shape in a critical position with the base of the rocket body and tape it to the rocket body. Rehash this to make another blade however this time on the opposite side. Bend the bit of each balance that takes after a triangle 90 degrees with the middle so each balance is at a right edge to its neighbor.

Step 3:

Tape this nose-cone to forestall any sort of air getting away. Evacuate the pencil and supplant it with a straw. At that point, blow into the straw to dispatch the rocket.

How It Works:

This movement makes an extraordinary investigation, a valuable building structure, and is ideal for the children with creative outlooks. Kids can see how changing points of the straw influences the separation went by rocket and how including folds or balances can influence this.

Precautions for Safety:

Best performed under parent supervision.

Observations:

_____

_____

_____

90. Cabbage Science

Things You'll Need:

- Plastic Bottle
- Knife
- Cabbage
- Strongly Acidic (Powdered Toilet Cleaner)
- Acidic (Vinegar)
- Weakly Acidic (Cream of Tartar)
- Neutral (Shampoo)
- Slightly Basic (Bicarbonate of Soda)
- Basic (Washing Soda)
- Strongly Basic (Dishwasher Liquid)
- 7 Cups

The Procedure:

Step 1:

Pick a plastic container and fill it half with water. At that point place these cabbage leaves in the bottle and screw the top on firmly. Shake the water bottle for a couple of seconds until the water turns profound purple. Leave the answer for cool.

Step 2:

Strain the arrangement and add adequate water to make the arrangement of 1L. Pick seven cups and in each cup place few family unit things in the accompanying request; strongly acidic, acidic, acidic, neutral, light basic, basic, strongly basic.

Step 3:

Presently half fill each cup with cabbage water and on the off chance that you put in them in the correct request as referenced it'll demonstrate following hues; cherry red (strongly acidic), pink-red (acidic), lilac (light acidic), purple (impartial/ neutral), blue (light basic), green (basic) and yellow (firmly basic).

How It Works:

All the things we eat or drink are acidic, and the things we use for cleaning are of basic nature. This is on the grounds that basic substances taste undesirable, yet a cleaning specialist for the most part should be basic to expel soil.

Precautions for Safety:

Handle the substances with care.

Observations:

_____

_____

_____

91. Soap & Pepper Experiment

Things You'll Need:

- Dish Soap
- Pepper
- Water
- Bowl

The Procedure:

Step 1:

Put some water in the base of a bowl and add some pepper in it.
Step 2:

Dip your finger in the center of bowl. You'll see the pepper flakes sticking to it.
Step 3:

Now dip your finger in liquid soap and then into pepper water. You'll observe the pepper going away to the edge of the bowl.

How It Works:

Dish cleanser is detailed to break the surface pressure of water, which is the reason it is so powerful on oily, filthy dishes. What's more, it wasn't until you added cleanser to the bowl that those "germs" were pursued away. This is the explanation adults are continually pestering you to wash your hands with cleanser!

Precautions for Safety:

Avoid touching your eyes unless you wash your hands.

Observations:

_____

_____

_____

92. Gummy Bears

Things You'll Need:

- 2 Small Bowls
- Salt
- Gummy Bears
- Water

The Procedure:

Step 1:

Heat water and dissolve maximum salt in it and then cool it in the refrigerator.

Step 2:

After that put some gummy bears in salted water and a few in normal water.

Step 3:

Keep them for several hours and then check the results. The salted ones will expand a bit whereas the ones in normal water will go under huge expansion. You can compare them with normal gummy bears.

How It Works:

This development of a dissolvable from one of lower fixation to higher focus is called osmosis.

The power behind that development of water is called osmotic weight.

Precautions for Safety:

Please do not carry out heating part without parent supervision.

Observations:

_____

_____

_____

93. Hidden Camera

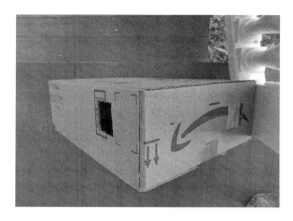

Things You'll Need:

- Wooden Box
- White Paper
- Dim Paper

The Procedure:

Step 1:

To begin, utilize a pencil's sharp highlight make a gap in the wooden box shorter side. Presently utilize a scissor to cut a square on the contrary side of the box, authentically inverse to the opening or gap you made first. Presently Use scissors to cut a square of white paper.

Step 2:

Spot this white sheet legitimately over the square you cut in the case, tape the edges of the sheet to the crate to fix it. Your camera is prepared. Take this camera box to a dull room and light up a light. Spread your head and pinhole camera with a cover or material.

Step 3:

Making such a camera is genuinely clear. Ensure the side with the opening is confronting the light and the side with a white sheet is confronting you. Hold your camera at a safe distance from your eyes and focus on the light. You'll see a topsy turvy picture of the light.

How It Works:

In a veritable camera, the point of convergence takes after the little hole you made in the wooden box and makes a retrogressive, up-side-down picture. Like the little opening, the point of convergence permits the light in. The white screen takes after a film in a certifiable camera, which has unique synthetic compounds on it. Exactly when the light hits the film, the synthetic substances start changing and change the visual picture into a photo.

Observations:

_____

_____

_____

94. Blind Spot

Things You'll Need:

- A Card
- Black Pen
-

The Procedure:

Step 1:

Hold the card at eye level about an a manageable distance away. Ensure that the cross is on the right.
Close your correct eye and take a gander at the cross with your left eye. Notice that you can likewise observe the speck.

Step 2:

Concentrate on the cross, yet know about the spot as you gradually bring the card toward your face. The dab will vanish, and afterward return, as you bring the card toward your face. Have a go at drawing the card nearer and farther to pinpoint precisely where this occurs.

Step 3:

Presently close your left eye and take a gander at the dab with your correct eye. This time the cross will vanish and return as you bring the card gradually toward your face.

How It Works:

The optic nerve—a heap of nerve strands that conveys messages from your eye to your mind—goes through one spot on the light-delicate coating, or retina, of your eye. In this recognize, your eye's retina has no light receptors. At the point when you hold the card so the light from the speck falls on this spot, you can't see the dab. The fovea is a zone of the retina that is thickly stuffed with light receptors, giving you the most honed vision.

Observations:

_____

_____

_____

95. Cool Crystals

Things You'll Need:

- Half Cup of Epsom salt
- Quarter Cup Hot Water
- Food Shading
- A Cup
- A Plate

The Procedure:

Step 1:

In the cup, measure out quarter cup Epsom salt and ¼ high temp water from the sink. Mix them together. On the off chance that all the salt doesn't disintegrate, heat the cup in the microwave for around 30 seconds.

Step 2:

At the point when all the salt is broken down, put a drop or two of food shading in the cup and mix to blend. Spot the cup in the fridge. Keep an eye on it each half hour or hour. Inside 4 hours, precious stones should frame in the base of the cup.

Step 3:

Scoop the gems onto a plate utilizing a fork. In the event that you need the precious stones to last more, put them in a container with a cover.

How It Works:

More salt can break down in boiling water than cold, so when the high temp water cools in the microwave, the Epsom salts make gems on the cup. The extraordinary state of Epsom salt particles makes them structure long gems that nearly look like needles. Various precious stones have various shapes. On the off chance that you take a gander at sugar or salt gems under an amplifying glass, you can see their cool precious stone shapes, as well

Precautions for Safety:

Perform under parent supervision.

Observations:

_____

_____

_____

96. Jello Lens

Things You'll Need:

- 1 Bundle of Gelatin Dessert Blend
3/4 cup of Water in a Mug
- Estimating Spoons & Estimating Cups
- Paper Towel
- Plate

The Procedure:

Step 1:

Start by warming the 3/4 cup of water in the microwave for a moment and a half. Empty the gelatin powder into a bowl, at that point pour the high temperature water over the powder. Combine them for two minutes.
Let the fluid cool for around ten minutes.

Step 2:

Spread a cutting board or a level plate with a paper towel. Scoop out some fluid with the little estimating spoons, at that point place them on the paper towel. To fill the bigger estimating cups, place the unfilled cups on the paper towel and cautiously pour the gelatin fluid in. Make an effort not to spill, this stuff makes an entirely clingy jumble to clean. Sit tight 4 hours for it to cool totally in fridge.

Step 3:

Following four hours, you can tenderly expel your focal points from the spoons and cups. Wash your hands in the sink before your touch them, wet hands mean the gelatin won't adhere to your skin while you are hauling them out. Add a little water to the base of a glass plate or bowl. At that point place a focal point inside, level side down. Move the bowl over various things to see them very close!

How It Works:

Focal points twist light as it travels through them. Your gelatin focal points work only a similar route as telescopes, magnifying instruments, optics, and eyeglasses!

Precautions for Safety:

Get a grown-up to assist you with managing close bubbling water!

Observations:

_____

_____

_____

97. Ice Fishing

Things You'll Need:

- Little Paper Cups
- Glass of Water
- String
- Little Stick
- Salt

The Procedure:

Step 1:

Top the cup off with water and spot it in the freezer. You can likewise utilize ice cubes from your freezer and skirt this progression.

Step 2:

At the point when the water is solidified, expel the ice from the cup. Put the ice in a bowl of water. The 3D shape will weave here and there in the water and afterward drift on the top.

Step 3:

Spot one finish of the string from the casting rod on head of the ice solid shape and sprinkle salt on the ice where the string is contacting. Watch as the water liquefies marginally and refreezes. After around 10 seconds, cautiously lift the ice solid shape out of the water with the casting rod. You got a fish (ice)

How It Works:

Conventional water freezes at (32° F). At the point when you add salt to water, it brings down the water's frosty temperature-it needs to get colder than 32° F to freeze. How much colder relies upon how much salt is blended in with the water. As the ice solid shape softens, it weakens the salt/water blend in the little pool; the point of solidification begins to return up once more. The ice refreezes, catching the string. When the ice 3D shape solidifies, you can raise it by lifting the string.

Observations:

---

98. Snow Globe

Things You'll Need:

- An Empty Jar with Lid
- Glycerin
- Water
- Glitter in White
- Decoration (Small Toys)

The Procedure:

Step 1:

Paste the toys or different designs to within the cover, ensuring the top can even now fit on the container. Fill the container most of the way with glycerin, at that point fill it nearly to the top with water, at that point mix to blend.

Step 2:

Include a modest quantity of sparkle. Mix with a spoon to test the 'day off, and include more until you get the whirlwinds or snowstorm you like. Top the container off the remainder of the way, until the water is simply over the head of the container.

Step 3:

Delicately put the cover on and screw it safely to the container. Wipe any water off the container, and put some heated glue or tape around the cover. Make the most of your snow globe!

How It Works:

Glycerin has a high consistency. Consistency is the way a fluid is, the way effectively it pours. Nectar and syrup have truly high viscosities; water and scouring liquor have low viscosities. Having a blend of water and glycerin implies the fluid inside your snow globe eases back the sparkle down as gravity pulls it down. This causes it look progressively like a snow.

Precautions for Safety:

Best performed under adult supervision.

Observations:

---

99. Gift Wrap

Things You'll Need:

- Shaving Cream
- Paper Towels
- Food Shading
- Computer Page
- Spoon
- Shallow Dish

The Procedure:

Step 1:

Utilizing a spoon, spread a far layer of shaving cream in the base of the dish. All you need is a shallow covering. Spot the outside of the shaving cream with food shading. Run the prongs of a fork through the
hues in a wavy manner. Attempt not twirling your hues or probably they will run together.

Step 2:

Lay your paper on head of the hued layer in the dish. Smooth the paper out over the shaving cream. Hold up for thirty seconds. Evacuate the paper and wipe the shaving cream off with a dry paper towel.

Step 3:

Permit your paper to dry. On the off chance that it twists, you can have a grown-up iron it level utilizing low warmth. Presently you can wrap your vacation endowments with your own enriched wrapping paper.

How It Works:

In science, retention is a compound or physical procedure where one substance takes in another substance. In this analysis, the shaving cream is engrossing the food shading and the paper at that point assimilates the hues. In result, we get multi-hued blessing wrap paper.

Precautions for Safety:

Avoid contact of shaving cream with your eyes.

Observations:

_____

_____

_____

100.Elephant Toothpaste

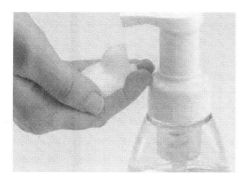

Things You'll Need:

- 16-oz Bottle
- Half Hydrogen Peroxide
- 1 Tablespoon of Dry Yeast
- 3 Tablespoons of Warm Water
- Fluid Dishwashing Cleanser
- Food Shading
- Little Cup
- Security Goggles

The Procedure:

Step 1:

An adult ought to painstakingly empty the hydrogen peroxide into the jug. Include 8 drops of your preferred food shading into the container.

Step 2:

Include around 1 tablespoon of fluid dish cleanser into the container and wash the jug around a piece to blend it.

Step 3:

In a different little cup, consolidate the warm water and the yeast together and blend for around 30 seconds. Empty the yeast water blend into the container (a pipe helps here) and watch the frothiness start.

How It Works:

The froth is uncommon in light of the fact that each small froth bubble is loaded up with oxygen. The yeast went about as an impetus to expel the oxygen from the hydrogen peroxide. Since it did this quick, it made parcels and loads of air pockets.

Precautions for Safety:

Hydrogen peroxide can disturb skin and eyes, so put on those security goggles.

Observations:

_____

_____

_____

101. Soft Turkey

Things You'll Need:

- 1 cup Water
- 1 Teaspoon Borax Powder
- Half Cup White Paste
- Markers
- 1 Nitrile Glove

The Procedure:

Step 1:

Put the glove in a tall glass, and stretch its opening over the edge of the glass. Pour the water and borax blend into the glove. Tie the glove like an inflatable.

Step 2:

Pour in half cup glue, at that point half cup water. Remove the glove from the glass and cautiously crunch it to blend the two. Empty 1 teaspoon borax into another half cup water, mix to blend.

Step 3:

Crunch the glove to blend all the fixings. Design your soft turkey!

How It Works:

The paste and borax combine to shape long chains of particles called polymers. As these polymers move around in the water, they stretch and remain together, making ooze!

Precautions for Safety:

Do not crunch the glove too hard.

Observations:

_____

_____

_____

CONCLUSION

Thank you for sparing some time of yours for reading this book and discovering the benefits of science and how it plays a role in our everyday lives. We hope that you enjoyed reading and performing these fun experiments with your little one's and that you've learnt a lot with these fun experiments.

If we look around in our surroundings we will see that everything around us has some science in it that we usually take for granted!

Printed in Great Britain
by Amazon

48179086R00124